CULTURES OF AMERICA

IRISH AMERICANS

By Janet Riehecky

Marshall Cavendish
New York • London • Toronto

Published by
Marshall Cavendish Corporation
2415 Jerusalem Avenue
P.O. Box 587
North Bellmore, New York 11710, U.S.A.

Edited, designed, and produced by Water Buffalo Books, Milwaukee

Project director: Mark Sachner
Art director: Sabine Beaupré
Picture researcher: Diane Laska
Editorial: Valerie Weber
Cover design: Lee Goldstein
Marshall Cavendish development editor: MaryLee Knowlton
Marshall Cavendish editorial director: Evelyn Fazio

Picture Credits: © Archive Photos: 38; © Archive Photos/Frank Capri/SAGA: 73 (bottom); © Archive Photos/S. E
SAGA: 75; Sabine Beaupré 1994: 7, 17; © M. Berman/H. Armstrong Roberts: 6; © The Bettmann Archive: 9, 10
23, 52, 73 (top), 74; Courtesy of the Conroy family: 40, 46, 47: © Culver Pictures, Inc.: 8, 18, 20, 24, 64 (top); I
Photo by Jane Gleeson: 51, 54; © Hazel Hankin: Cover, 1, 4, 5, 26, 28, 29, 30, 31, 33, 35, 39, 41, 42, 43, 45, 48,
55, 57 (bottom), 61; Irish Fest Photo by Paul H. Henning: 56; Irish Fest Photo by Martin Hintz: 50, 57 (top); © E
Bettmann: 36, 59, 64 (bottom), 65, 70; © UPI/Bettmann: 11, 15, 16, 25, 32, 62, 67, 69, 71, 72; © Catherine Urs
Armstrong Roberts: 58

Library of Congress Cataloging-in-Publication Data

Riehecky, Janet, 1953-
    Irish Americans / Janet Riehecky.
        p.   cm. — (Cultures of America)
    Includes bibliographical references and index.
    ISBN 1-85435-780-8 (set). — ISBN 1-85435-783-2
    1. Irish Americans—Juvenile literature. I. Title. II. Series.
    E184.I6R54   1995
    305.891'62073—dc20   94-12604
                                                                        CIP
                                                                        AC

To PS – MS
For my son, Patrick: May you always be proud of the part of you that's Irish – JR

IRISH AMERICANS

By Janet Riehecky

Marshall Cavendish
New York • London • Toronto

Published by
Marshall Cavendish Corporation
2415 Jerusalem Avenue
P.O. Box 587
North Bellmore, New York 11710, U.S.A.

Edited, designed, and produced by Water Buffalo Books, Milwaukee

Project director: Mark Sachner
Art director: Sabine Beaupré
Picture researcher: Diane Laska
Editorial: Valerie Weber
Cover design: Lee Goldstein
Marshall Cavendish development editor: MaryLee Knowlton
Marshall Cavendish editorial director: Evelyn Fazio

Picture Credits: © Archive Photos: 38; © Archive Photos/Frank Capri/SAGA: 73 (bottom); © Archive Photos/S. Hood/ SAGA: 75; Sabine Beaupré 1994: 7, 17; © M. Berman/H. Armstrong Roberts: 6; © The Bettmann Archive: 9, 10, 12, 14, 23, 52, 73 (top), 74; Courtesy of the Conroy family: 40, 46, 47: © Culver Pictures, Inc.: 8, 18, 20, 24, 64 (top); Irish Fest Photo by Jane Gleeson: 51, 54; © Hazel Hankin: Cover, 1, 4, 5, 26, 28, 29, 30, 31, 33, 35, 39, 41, 42, 43, 45, 48, 49, 53, 55, 57 (bottom), 61; Irish Fest Photo by Paul H. Henning: 56; Irish Fest Photo by Martin Hintz: 50, 57 (top); © Reuters/ Bettmann: 36, 59, 64 (bottom), 65, 70; © UPI/Bettmann: 11, 15, 16, 25, 32, 62, 67, 69, 71, 72; © Catherine Ursillo/H. Armstrong Roberts: 58

Library of Congress Cataloging-in-Publication Data

Riehecky, Janet, 1953-
    Irish Americans / Janet Riehecky.
        p.   cm. — (Cultures of America)
    Includes bibliographical references and index.
    ISBN 1-85435-780-8 (set). — ISBN 1-85435-783-2
    1. Irish Americans—Juvenile literature. I. Title. II. Series.
    E184.I6R54   1995
    305.891'62073—dc20   94-12604
                                                        CIP
                                                        AC

To PS – MS
For my son, Patrick: May you always be proud of the part of you that's Irish – JR

CONTENTS

Introduction   4

Chapter One: Leaving a Homeland: A Desperate People   6

The First Irish Americans • A Conquered Nation • Life in a Mud Hut • Coping •
Resentment, Rebellion, and Compromise • The Potato Famine • The British Response •
The Long Good-bye

**Chapter Two: Life in a New Land: America: Where the Streets Are
Paved with Gold**   16

Leaving Ireland • Traveling Steerage • Arrival • "Mud undher th' pavement" • Poverty
and Prejudice • "No Irish Need Apply" • "If There's a Way into the Woods . . ." •
A Force to Be Reckoned with • Assimilation

Chapter Three: Family and Community: The Irish American Family   26

An Intense Family Loyalty • The Family Unit • Expressing Affection • Siblings •
Patterns of Communication • Delayed Marriages • Family Goals • "Who Do They
Think They Are?" • Neighborhoods • The Future

**Chapter Four: Religion and Celebrations: Irish America
and the Catholic Church**   36

Roots in the Old Country • The Irish Immigrant Church • Parochial Schools • Social
Services • The Other Catholics • The Middle Class and the Catholic Church • Dissent •
The 1990s • The Sacraments • The Future

**Chapter Five: Customs, Expressions, and Hospitality:
Culture and Traditions**   48

Hospitality • Clannishness • Celtic People • A Land of Poets • Celtic Art • Dance •
Music • Celebrations • Passion for the Past • Concern for the Future • Being Irish
Means More than Drinking Green Beer

**Chapter Six: Contributions to American Culture: Irish American
Achievements and Influence**   62

Irish American Politicians • Political Power • Patronage • A Rich Legacy • Labor
Unions • Builders of America • The Irish Mob • Professional Sports • "There's No
Business Like Show Business" • Literature • Business and Industry • An Intangible Legacy

Chronology, Glossary, Further Reading, and Index   76

INTRODUCTION

Every year on March 17, special celebrations occur all over the United States: In New York City, the Empire State Building displays green lights in its windows; in San Antonio, Texas, and Chicago, the citizens throw green dye in their rivers; Briarwood Beach, Ohio, has declared the day a legal holiday; there are parades across the nation, and people everywhere make sure to wear something green. On St. Patrick's Day, everyone tries to be a little bit Irish, but twenty-three million people in the United States of America are proud to be Irish during the rest of the year, too. Yet it wasn't always that way. In the mid-1800s, when the first large wave of Irish immigrants came to America, they were greeted with fear and suspicion.

Irish immigrants, fleeing a blight that had destroyed their main food supply, arrived on the shores of North America with little to offer. Most were weak with starvation, many were ill, and nearly all were poverty-stricken. U.S.-born Americans were quick to exploit this large labor force that couldn't afford to say no to any job, but they shunned any other contact with the Irish immigrants. Yet the courage and indomitable will of the Irish could not be crushed. They had survived a thousand years of British oppression. Once they experienced the freedom of America, there would be no stopping them. The story of how Irish Americans overcame poverty and prejudice to win a place of honor in this country is an inspiring and heart-wrenching story. It is one all Americans can look to with pride.

Two farmers stack hay in County Donegal, Ireland. Life might be hard, but the beautiful, green Irish countryside helps compensate.

CHAPTER ONE

LEAVING A HOMELAND
A DESPERATE PEOPLE

In 1846, a visitor to Ireland stopped in the village of Skibbereen. He sent a letter back to England, describing what he found in one of the cottages:

> . . . six famished and ghastly skeletons, to all appearance dead, huddled in a corner, their sole covering what seemed to be a ragged horse cloth. . . . I approached in horror and found by a low moaning that they were alive, they were in fever — four children, a woman, and what had once been a man. . . . In a few minutes I was surrounded by at least 200 of such phantoms, such frightful spectres as no words can describe. By far the greater number were delirious either from famine or fever. . . . Within 500 yards of the Cavalry Station at Skibbereen, the dispensary doctor found seven wretches lying, unable to move, under the same clock — one had been dead many hours, but the others were unable to move, either themselves or the corpse.

In the decade from 1845 to 1855, this same scene was repeated over and over again in villages throughout Ireland. Hundreds of thousands of Irish people were dying. The cause was not war or some unidentifiable and untreatable disease. These people were starving to death — starving because the potatoes they relied upon for their survival were rotting in the fields.

The Irish potato famine and the events that led up to it comprise one of the most overwhelming catastrophes that has ever struck any nation. The famine devastated the population of that country and changed the character of its people. It also had a tremendous impact on the United States. For to escape that famine, nearly two million Irish people emigrated to North America.

The First Irish Americans

Irish people had been emigrating to North America since it was first open to colonization, but those who went before the 1800s

In the 1920s, chiefly Catholic Ireland was freed from British rule. Chiefly Protestant Northern Ireland remains part of the United Kingdom.

King Henry II of England (1133-1189). His invasion of Ireland in 1171 led to nearly one thousand years of English rule over the Irish.

were mainly middle class. They blended into existing settlements without too much difficulty, using their skills and financial resources to build their communities. Those of the lower classes who emigrated earned praise for their strength and willingness to work hard.

In the mid-1800s, all that changed. The thin trickle of immigrants was transformed to a flood, and the type of immigrant changed from the hardy adventurer or prosperous shopkeeper to the poorest Irish peasants. In the decade from 1845 to 1855, nearly two million Irish people braved tremendous hardships, leaving the homeland they loved for an uncertain life in a country thousands of miles away, driven out by hunger.

A Conquered Nation

Ireland has always been considered one of the most beautiful nations in Europe. It is a small country, about the size of the state of Maine, located at the western edge of Europe and the eastern edge of the Atlantic Ocean. Abundant rainfall has produced a grassy, rolling countryside of vivid green, which has given the island its nickname, the Emerald Isle. In the 1800s, Ireland was covered by large, productive farms called estates. However, the vast majority of those estates were not owned by the Irish; instead, they were owned by the English. Ireland was a conquered nation and had been since 1171, when King Henry II of England landed his troops in southern Ireland and conquered the land. English colonists followed the English soldiers, and so began centuries of English rule and oppression in Ireland.

During the centuries after the English conquest, the English confiscated Irish land and passed strict laws limiting the rights of the Irish people. After King Henry VIII of England broke with the Catholic Church in 1534, he and his successors directed those laws specifically against Irish Catholics. The laws, known as Penal Laws, prohibited Catholics from voting, owning land, holding public office, or educating their children in the Catholic faith. The Catholic mass was prohibited, and a bounty was placed on all Catholic priests, who were executed or exiled if caught. At one time, the death sentence was imposed on anyone performing a marriage between a Protestant and a Catholic. Even the Irish language, Gaelic, was banned. These laws were all repealed by 1829, but by then the character of the Irish people and their way of life had been substantially affected.

By the mid-1800s, the overwhelming majority of the Irish people were peasants living in small villages on the estates of English landlords. The English represented less than 1 percent of the population, yet they owned more than 80 percent of the land. The Irish peasants were not permitted to own the land they lived on or the homes they lived in. They rented the land their ancestors had owned and planted crops that belonged to English landlords. Their lives were ones of abject poverty, with little hope they could ever achieve anything better.

A picturesque thatched cottage in the Irish countryside in the 1890s. Few Irish peasants in the mid-1800s would have lived in such "luxury."

Life in a Mud Hut

In 1839, a French traveler named de Beaumont described the impact of a visit to Ireland on him: "I saw the American Indian in his forests and the black slave in his chains, and I believed that I was seeing in their pitiful condition the most extreme form of human misery, but that was before I knew the lot of poor Ireland."

A British commission investigating the conditions in Ireland in the early 1800s concluded that the Irish laboring class endured greater suffering than any other people in Europe.

The housing for Irish peasants was worse than any slum today. A few landlords built cottages for their tenants, and some Irish peasants were able to build stone cottages for themselves, but the majority lived in one-room mud huts. Ireland's soil contains many rocks, remnants of the great glaciers that once covered the island. The peasants took a few wooden planks and covered them with dirt and rocks to shape walls, then covered the

HEDGE SCHOOLS

The Irish people have always loved learning and treasured knowledge. Thus, the Penal Laws prohibiting Irish Catholics from attending school, running schools, or sending their children abroad to be educated were particularly resented. The Irish people, used to avoiding the law, responded by starting illegal schools. These schools became known as *hedge schools* because they usually met outdoors, concealed from English eyes by a large hedge. Hedge schools, often run by Catholic priests, taught lessons in the forbidden Gaelic language and emphasized poetry, Latin, and Greek. The quality of the instruction was so good that students smuggled out of the country were accepted into some of the best colleges in continental Europe.

PEAT BOGS

The one blessing for Irish peasants living in mud huts was heat. Fifteen percent of Ireland is composed of peat bogs, thick layers of decayed plants that can be cut into bricks, dried, and burned for fuel. Ireland's temperature is naturally mild. Ocean currents traveling across the Atlantic from the Gulf of Mexico keep the temperature moderate most of the time. In the summer, the average temperature is sixty degrees Fahrenheit; in the winter, forty degrees Fahrenheit. So, to stay warm, Irish peasants simply needed to dig a supply of peat and stack it by their cottages, much as a settler in America might have laid in a supply of firewood. Only an unusually severe winter would add cold to the hardships the peasants already suffered.

structure with thatch. An opening was left for the door, but there weren't any windows. Nor were there any bathrooms. Furniture was a rarity: One 1837 survey counted 10 beds, 93 chairs, and 243 stools among a population of nine thousand people. A family of eight, twelve, even fifteen people would crowd into one of these small dwellings — and often share it with a pig!

There was no incentive for Irish families to try to build anything better, even if they had the resources to do so, because any improvements that an Irish family made on the land, including building a cottage, belonged solely to the landlord. No compensation of any kind was given to the Irish tenant for the work done. In fact, the rent might be raised because of the improvements. In addition, the landlord had the right to evict tenants at any time, for any reason. If the landlord found someone willing to pay a higher rent than the family living on the land or simply wanted the land for another purpose, he or she could evict the tenants without any notice.

In the early 1800s, the typical Irish family rented a few acres of land to farm. Most of the land would be used for the rent crop of wheat, oats, barley, hay, wool, or cotton. The family would make no money on that crop. It would be shipped to England for the use of the English landlord. The Irish family was permitted a small portion of the land to grow food, and its whole survival was dependent on that small crop.

Problems arose as Ireland's population grew. Sons and daughters married young, often at age sixteen or seventeen. When they did, the family split the land they rented so that the newly married couple would have a place to live. Irish families loved children and tended to have many of them. Families with

An Irish family sharing a frugal meal, 1920. Even into the beginning of the twentieth century, many Irish families had few resources available to them.

TUMBLING A COTTAGE

Eviction of tenants and the immediate destruction of their homes became so commonplace that it was given a name, *tumbling a cottage*. A sheriff and several deputies would receive orders to evict a tenant from a landlord or his or her agent. They would travel to the property and order the residents to give up possession of the land. Often the tenants had only minutes to gather their possessions before the sheriff and his men tore the roof from the cottage and collapsed the walls. Some teams had so much practice tumbling cottages that they were able to demolish an entire home in less than an hour. No provision was made for the dispossessed family. They sometimes found shelter in ditches or caves, but usually they died of hunger and exposure within weeks.

Irish celebrations have traditionally included spirited dances, such as the Irish jig. Sharing fun and fellowship helped the Irish forget their troubles.

six, ten, even fifteen children were common. This was encouraged by the Catholic Church and by the fact that parents had to rely on their children to care for them in their old age. The acreage suitable for farming was limited, and family holdings were split again and again. The land became overpopulated, and many found themselves trying to survive by farming barely a quarter acre of land.

Coping

There were few options for those dissatisfied with their lives. Some emigrated, but these were mostly middle-class Irish, as they were the only ones who could afford the passage to Canada or the U.S. Some looked for other jobs, but Belfast and Dublin were the only cities of any size, and they offered

only a few factory jobs. Some coastal villages attempted to make a living fishing, but the treacherous currents of the Atlantic made that way of life even more risky than farming. The island produced rich crops of wheat, oats, barley, rye, wool, and cotton, but all the profits went to the English landlords — and all these resources were exported to England.

The Irish coped by pulling together as families and communities. Social gatherings held great importance. Any excuse was sufficient for a celebration. A whole village would gather together for weddings or wakes, and people would walk miles to attend a fair. Sporting events such as hurling (a game that resembles lacrosse) were popular and so were races. When a family needed a new cottage, everyone in the community worked together to raise it. Those gatherings and other social events were marked by work alternating with singing, dancing, storytelling, and drinking.

Good manners and hospitality were very important to the Irish people. Their rights had been taken away, but not their dignity. No matter how limited the food, no stranger was turned away empty-handed, and no woman feared molestation as she walked through the countryside. Irish peasants were also sociable, willing and eager to talk for hours. A clever tongue was greatly admired, and storytelling was a treasured art. Pubs were popular gathering places, where frequently the drink was less important than the company.

Resentment, Rebellion, and Compromise

But the friendliness and hospitality of the Irish peasants did not extend to the English among them. Fierce resentment and hatred of the English burned in the hearts of most of the Irish people. The Irish gave their loyalty to their faith, their family, and their friends, rather than to the government in London. These feelings shaped the way Irish people led their lives at home and influenced their dealings with public officials.

The Irish rarely went to court to settle a dispute. Any attempt by Irish people to obtain justice through the court system failed, as lawyers, judges, and juries were nearly always English Protestants who blatantly displayed prejudice and favoritism. The Irish Catholic peasants learned to practice deception, and they became experts at finding loopholes in the law. Open rebellion, secret societies, murders, and night raids against landlords and informers happened frequently as the Irish attempted to expel the English and regain Irish freedom. By the mid-1800s, these efforts, along with attempts at compro-

THE ENGLISH LANDLORDS

English landlords generally lived in England rather than Ireland. Though there were a few good landlords who cared about their tenants, most English landlords viewed their Irish estates purely as a source of income, and their concern all too often revolved around producing higher and higher profits. Many visited their Irish estates only once or twice a year. Some never visited at all, relying on an agent to run the estate. Most English believed that the Irish were an inferior race, and the suffering of unseen Irish peasants was of little concern — and no laws protected those peasants.

Mrs. Gerrard of the village of Ballinglass, Ireland, was a typical example of how cruel an English landlord could be. In 1846, Mrs. Gerrard decided it would be more profitable to turn her Irish estate into a grazing farm. Seventy-six families, three hundred people, lived in solidly built, well-kept homes on her estate. They had worked hard, reclaiming about four hundred acres of bog so that the land could be farmed. Yet when Mrs. Gerrard decided they had to go, they had no choice and no recourse. While the people desperately tried to gather some possessions, the roofs were torn from their houses and the walls collapsed. The homeless tenants took refuge in ditches, but Mrs. Gerrard wanted them off her estate. The next day the sheriff and his men drove them from the ditches.

The potato was an ideal crop for Irish peasants to raise. It was inexpensive, nutritious, and required only spadework to plant and harvest.

mise, peaceful coexistence, even collaboration with the British and conversion to Protestantism, had become a way of life for many Irish.

In the mid-1800s, Ireland was ripe for some sort of disaster, and disaster struck.

The Potato Famine

For many years, the potato was all that separated the Irish peasant from starvation. It was cheap, easily grown on the small plot of land peasants were allowed to use for themselves, and required little attention besides planting and harvesting. The potato is amazingly nutritious, containing essential carbohydrates, protein, vitamins, and minerals, and it can be cooked in an almost limitless variety of ways. For decades, the majority of Irish peasants lived exclusively on potatoes, their diet supplemented only by cow's milk and occasional turnips. Then, in 1845, disease attacked the potato crop.

It started slowly. First predictions were that 1845 would see a bumper crop of potatoes. But as the crop was harvested, disaster struck. Many fields yielded large numbers of potatoes, but there was something wrong with them. Sometimes the potatoes looked healthy coming out of the ground, but then they turned black days or even hours later. Sometimes the potatoes rotted right in the ground. In field after field, entire crops of potatoes dissolved to black, sticky pulp.

As the stench of rotting potatoes swept over the land, panic took hold. The Irish peasants didn't dare eat the crops they raised for rent. Agents monitored the growth of the crops and the landlord would evict the peasants for even a small shortage — and the homeless almost invariably died of starvation and exposure. The Irish peasants paid their rent and went hungry. During the whole of the famine, while the Irish people were starving, shipload after shipload of food left Ireland to be exported to England.

The next ten years produced one of the worst disasters any nation has ever experienced. The blight ruined the potato crop every year, with the exception of 1847. Estimates vary widely about the number of people who died during that time, but it is likely that over 2.5 million starved or died of related diseases during the famine. And the suffering of those who lived cannot even be imagined.

The British Response

The British government offered some minor assistance, such as soup kitchens and public works projects, but they were unable and unwilling to provide the massive assistance necessary to feed eight million Irish peasants. Many British government officials felt that the famine wasn't really that bad, so they required the Irish people to give up all their possessions in order to get public aid, thinking this would force them to rely on their own resources instead of British charity.

If anything, however, the disaster had been understated, not exaggerated, and because of the harsh British economic policies, the Irish had no other resources to fall back on. Many thousands of Irish peasants gave up everything they had, and any hope for a future, for the sake of eating that day.

Because most of the English regarded the Irish as inferior, there was little sympathy in England for the starving Irish peasants who had rebelled so often against British rule. British government officials piously stated that the famine was God's way of reducing the surplus population in Ireland. One even worried that the famine wouldn't kill enough of them. As hunger gripped the nation, emigration seemed the only solution for many.

The Long Good-bye

It was a difficult and painful decision for the Irish to consider emigration. Whatever they felt about the British government, they loved Ireland. And the separation from their village, family, and friends was heart wrenching. Those leaving knew it was unlikely they'd ever again see those they left behind. Often a village would hold a wake the night before an individual or a family planned to leave, as if they were dying instead of emigrating.

But hope and despair drove hundreds of thousands to make that choice. There was no future in Ireland, but there might be one in America.

An Irish immigrant family headed for New York in 1926. Though travel conditions had greatly improved by the 1900s, it was still heartbreaking to leave Ireland.

In the nineteenth and twentieth centuries, thousands of immigrants flooded major ports such as New York, Boston, and New Orleans. This 1923 photo shows immigrants coming to Boston.

CHAPTER TWO

LIFE IN A NEW LAND
AMERICA: WHERE THE STREETS ARE PAVED WITH GOLD

In George Potter's book, *To the Golden Door: The Story of the Irish in Ireland and America*, he tells of an Irish railway worker writing to his family back in Ireland. The immigrant told his family of the wonderful opportunities and abundant food available in the United States. But when he showed the letter to his employer, his boss was puzzled. "Why do you say that you have meat three times a week, when you have it three times a day?" the boss asked. The immigrant answered, "Sure, if you wrote that, they'd never believe it."

An Irish peasant in the early 1800s might have meat once a year. To those peasants, America sounded like a promised land, flowing with milk and honey. Letters from emigrants who had crossed the Atlantic told of work opportunities, plentiful food, and freedom from political oppression. The emigrants often provided proof of how well they were doing by enclosing money for their struggling families. Letters were shared throughout the close-knit villages so that nearly every Irish peasant knew about the opportunities available across the ocean.

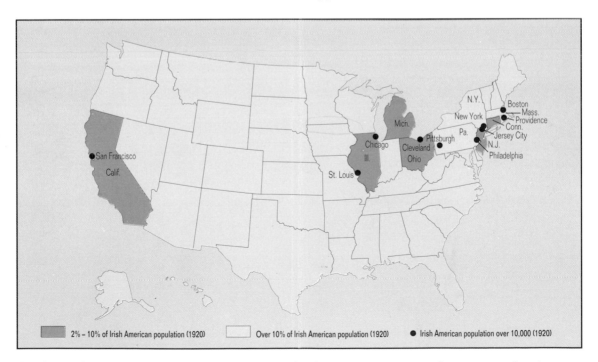

2% – 10% of Irish American population (1920) Over 10% of Irish American population (1920) ● Irish American population over 10,000 (1920)

By the early 1900s, Irish Americans had made their move west, in the process fanning out throughout the Midwest, well beyond the eastern cities where they had initially entered the U.S.

No matter how crowded and dangerous the conditions on an immigrant ship might be, the first sight of America raised hope among the passengers who survived the ocean crossing.

When the potato famine struck, these letters provided the only hope for thousands of Irish families.

Leaving Ireland

Faced with starvation, thousands and thousands of Irish peasants decided emigration was their only chance, but the dream of a better life frequently became a nightmare. Few Irish peasants had ever traveled beyond their own village. They knew nothing of how to make travel arrangements or what to do once they landed in America. And there were many people ready and eager to take advantage of their ignorance.

Some emigrants were cheated before they even started — the tickets they bought were forgeries. Some emigrants sold nearly everything they owned to be able to afford their tickets, so they arrived in America penniless.

Many sold themselves as indentured servants, who were required to work an average of seven years for whomever paid their passage money. Some had friends or relatives in North America who could send them passage money, but even those had to face the horror of the crossing itself. Ship companies wanted to make huge profits transporting emigrants; they were not concerned about making the trip safe or comfortable.

Traveling Steerage

Ships from North America had been delivering goods from Canada and the United States to Europe for many years. Rather than returning empty, captains sold passages in steerage to Canada and the U.S. Soon the holds that had held lumber and cotton housed Irish immigrants seeking escape. And as little money as possible had been spent making those holds suitable for human habitation. Traveling steerage, as this kind of passage was called, could be endured only because it was better than the conditions the Irish had left behind. An Irishman named Stephen deVere described what he saw during his own passage across the Atlantic:

> Before the emigrant has been a week at sea he is an altered man. How can it be otherwise? Hundreds of poor people, men, women, and children, of all ages, from the drivelling idiot of ninety to the babe just born, huddled together without light, without air, wallowing in filth and breathing a fetid atmosphere, sick in body, dispirited in heart, the fevered patient lying . . . in sleeping places so narrow as almost to deny them the power of indulging, by a change of position, the natural restlessness of their diseases; by the agonized raving disturbing those around, and predisposing them through the effects of imagination, to imbibe the contagion; living without food or medicine . . . dying without the voice of spiritual consolation, and burying in the deep without the rites of the church.

In the worst ships, hundreds of people were crammed into an area designed to hold thirty or forty. No bathrooms were available. Often the immigrants were not allowed up on deck for the entire voyage. The captain was supposed to provide minimal provisions for those who were unable to bring their own food, but frequently he did not. Few Irish emigrants had ever been on the sea before, and many became violently seasick. And it was a rare ship that didn't contain passengers with typhoid or other contagious diseases crowded in with the other passengers. The

COFFIN SHIPS

So many people died during the voyages to North America that the ships carrying immigrants were soon unofficially christened *coffin ships*. The *Elizabeth and Sarah* was a typical example of a coffin ship.

The *Elizabeth and Sarah*, an eighty-six-year-old ship, left Ireland in July of 1846 carrying 276 passengers. For this many people, it should have stocked 12,532 gallons of water; instead, it carried only 8,700 gallons. British law required the captain to provide seven pounds of food for each passenger for each week of the trip, but there were no provisions of any kind given to the passengers on this voyage. During the eight weeks it took the ship to cross the Atlantic, the passengers suffered the agonies of starvation and thirst. Added to this was the fact that there were only thirty-two berths available for the 276 passengers. Thus, 244 people had no space allotted to them except the floor of the hold — not the most comfortable spot considering there were no toilets and many of the passengers were seasick. Forty-two people on the *Elizabeth and Sarah* died during that crossing.

crossing might take from one to three months, and during that time some historians estimate that an average of one out of ten Irish emigrants died, their bodies pitched into the Atlantic Ocean. But one out of four was still dying at home.

Arrival

Things did not get better after the ships docked in North America. Most of the

Irish American journalist Finley Peter Dunne. Dunne's essays and stories etched vivid pictures of every aspect of the lives of Irish immigrants.

because the laws regulating those ships were stricter, but there was still overcrowding, disease, and hunger. Irish immigrants landing in the major ports of Boston, New York, and New Orleans were often just as bad off as those docking in Canada.

Still, Irish immigrants preferred to go to the United States because it was an independent country free of the hated British rule. And, at that time, the United States was also more prosperous, with more jobs available. In fact, most of the Irish immigrants who landed in Canada immediately moved again to the United States, often crossing the border illegally.

But the help the Irish immigrants needed was unavailable whether they settled in Canada or in the United States. Everywhere the immigrants turned, their sheer numbers and extreme poverty overwhelmed the resources available. There simply wasn't enough hospital space for all the sick, and there wasn't adequate housing or food or jobs for the healthy. For example, in 1847, the quarantine hospital on Grosse Isle, Canada, coped with 2500 seriously ill Irish immigrants — overflowing a space designed to hold 150 people. In Boston and New York, thousands of Irish immigrants flooded those cities' inexpensive housing until three and four families crowded into space inadequate for one, and shacks and shanties were erected in backyards and alleyways all over those cities. The overcrowding helped spread disease and crime. Many Irish immigrants survived the famine and the ocean crossing, only to die within a few weeks after reaching North America.

poorest Irish immigrants traveled first to Canada, as the British government kept fares on British ships to Quebec low to encourage emigration and to help populate their colony there. But the low fares they received caused ship owners to skimp even more than usual on the provisions they were supposed to provide for their passengers. Ship after ship arrived in Canada carrying hundreds of starving, sick people, people who needed immediate help rather than sturdy homesteaders who could build up the colony.

Conditions were a little better on U.S. ships traveling directly to the United States

RUNNERS

Irish immigrants were often "helped" to find accommodations by con artists called runners. Runners met ships carrying Irish immigrants. They often sported green neckties and spoke with Irish brogues to gain the confidence of the bewildered new arrivals. They stole the newcomer's luggage, claiming that it would be stored for the immigrant, and led the poor Irish immigrants to rooming houses where they were charged outrageous sums of money.

One immigrant who simply asked for directions was told that the stagecoach to his destination wouldn't come for two days. He was then hustled into a room and told to wait until the man returned. Two days later, the immigrant timidly ventured out onto the streets. There he learned that he was just twenty minutes from his destination — and that he was being charged for his stay more than New York's most luxurious hotel would have charged.

"Mud undher th' pavement"

In Ireland, the Irish peasants had suffered starvation and political oppression, but they did so in the beautiful Irish countryside, surrounded by congenial neighbors and loving family. Now they found themselves living in tenement houses or shacks in the slums of large cities. They were surrounded by garbage and filth and resented by the so-called native Americans. Their disillusionment was almost as difficult to bear as the poverty and discrimination they faced. They had expected a beautiful land, where the streets were "paved with gold," but as Mr. Dooley, a fictional Irish immigrant created by Irish American journalist Finley Peter Dunne, put it, "Whin I'd been here a week, I seen that there was nawthin' but mud undher th' pavement."

Poverty and Prejudice

The typical Irish immigrant family crowded into a filthy cellar or a squalid tenement house in the slums of a large city, often sharing quarters with several other families. While the flimsy construction, poor maintenance, and general filth did not shock the Irish because it was not much different from their mud huts in Ireland, the wretchedness of these places shocked the government officials that occasionally inspected them. Cellars flooded often, sometimes leaving as much as four inches of standing water. There were no laws regulating ventilation, lighting, or sanitary facilities, so these were minimal or nonexistent. In fact, there didn't even have to be a supply of water available to the tenants in these slums.

There were, however, always dance halls and taverns nearby, inviting the despairing Irish immigrant to slide further into a life of degradation. Disease and crime ravaged these communities. At one point, the average Irish immigrant could expect to live only fourteen years after coming to the United States, and infant mortality in the slums ran to a horrifying 80 percent.

In addition to this, Catholic Irish immigrants faced overt hostility from the Protestant majority in America, many of whom thought that Catholics wanted to bring the United States under the Pope's control. Convents and churches were vandalized and even burned to the ground. Catholics were verbally and physically attacked. And, just as the English had done in Ireland, Americans passed laws restricting the rights of Catholics. New Hampshire required them to swear an oath against the Pope and excluded them from holding political office. Pennsylvania imposed a special tax on them, and New York prohibited Catholics from bearing firearms.

"No Irish Need Apply"

Irish immigrants also had a difficult time when they tried to find jobs. Before the famine migration, Irish workers were welcomed by employers and respected for their ability to work hard. Now there were more workers than jobs, and instead of sturdy, strong peasants, these immigrants were sick and weak. U.S.-born American citizens were afraid that Irish immigrants carried contagious diseases, and many believed the British propaganda that Irish people were all stupid and lazy. Soon "No Irish Need Apply" signs appeared on rooming houses in the better parts of town and at better places of employment. Only the most menial, difficult, and dangerous jobs were open to Irish immigrants. The Irish cleaned stables, unloaded ships, pushed carts, and worked on hazardous construction jobs.

"If there's a way into the woods . . ."

Prejudice, poverty, and disease threatened to overwhelm Irish immigrants as they tried to make new lives for themselves in America. But an old Irish adage states, "If there's a way into the woods, there's a way out." The Irish had always been fighters, and they weren't about to give up now.

The Irish immigrants had two advantages over most other immigrant groups. First of all, they spoke the language. Because of the British government's ban on their native tongue of Gaelic, most Irish immigrants spoke English. This made it easier for them to gain some kinds of work, and it also made it easier for them to function in society. They also understood the American political and court systems, which were similar to Ireland's. As a result, one of the first inroads Irish immigrants made into American life was in the area of politics.

A Force to Be Reckoned with

Sheer numbers at first made the Irish valuable to politicians. By 1850, 26 percent of the population of New York City had been born in Ireland, and 20 percent of Boston was Irish. Their votes could swing an election one way or another. For centuries in Ireland, the Irish had regarded the law imposed on them by British invaders as something to be manipulated. So, the Irish had no moral objection to selling their votes. To them, voting for someone in return for a job was a fair and practical trade and was seen as something of value exchanged for something of value. Once in the States, the Irish affiliated themselves with the Democratic party and worked hard to get Democrats elected to office. Local politicians kept their end of the bargain and provided jobs for Irish immigrants in the police forces and fire departments. Gradually, too, Irish immigrants, now naturalized American citizens or second-generation Irish Americans, began holding appointed and then elected positions within the government.

The Irish immigrants also found a place for themselves in the army. Irish emigrants had traditionally sought military careers after leaving Ireland. When the Civil War began in 1861, the Irish enlisted in large numbers. The war gave them a chance to prove their patriotism and also demonstrated to fellow soldiers that the Irish were not lazy, stupid,

THE FORD FAMILY

As Irish immigrants looked for jobs, surprisingly few chose to head west and become homesteaders, a path that other immigrant groups had followed with great success. For many, this was an economic decision. It took money to move west and set up a farm, and few had any money at all. In Boston, some Irish immigrants couldn't even leave the city because they couldn't afford the toll charged to cross the bridges. Many, too, felt that the land had betrayed them in Ireland, and they were unwilling to risk crop failure in the U.S. Also, growing vast fields of corn or wheat required different skills than those needed to grow a small plot of potatoes. Finally, the Irish immigrant disliked the lifestyle of farming families in the States.

The Irish were a neighborly, talkative people, and having one's nearest neighbors miles away was just too lonesome a way to live. For all these reasons, Irish immigrants became primarily urban dwellers.

Among the few Irish immigrants who did head west was a man named John Ford, a small farmer from County Cork. His wife died shortly after their arrival in Canada, but John pressed on, eventually emigrating to the United States and settling in Detroit. Ford settled on a small farm in the Michigan wilderness rather than in the city, but his grandson would change the lives of both city and country dwellers forever. His grandson was Henry Ford, inventor of the mass-produced automobile.

The son of an Irish immigrant, Henry Ford (shown here in 1896 with his first car off the assembly line in Dearborn, Michigan) changed the lives of all Americans with his invention of the automobile.

Some Irish coal miners fought back against the exploitation by the mine owners by forming secret societies. This illustration shows a meeting of the Molly Maguires, an organization that was alleged to have used intimidation, sabotage, and even murder to gain concessions from bosses.

drunken bums as they were labeled. Many U.S.-born American citizens came away from the war impressed by the courage and bravery the Irish displayed on the battlefield.

Irish immigrants and second-generation Irish Americans sought to end the exploitation of their people by joining labor unions and forming secret societies. Few, if any, safety regulations protected the Irish who built canals, laid railroad track, and dug coal. The Irish workers might toil fifteen hours a day to earn only fifty cents at these dangerous jobs. Hundreds of thousands of them died, and there was no compensation for injuries or deaths that occurred on the job. The Irish were used to being exploited like this; the British had done it to them for centuries. And they already had the skills to fight back. Secret societies such as the Molly Maguires

used guerrilla warfare and violent tactics against mine owners and other industrialists. Using political clout and this kind of pressure eventually enabled Irish Americans to improve working conditions not just for themselves, but for all laboring people in America.

Some Irish Americans found their ticket out of the slums through sports. Boxing and baseball were dominated by Irish American athletes in the later half of the nineteenth and the early twentieth centuries. As Americans cheered and admired those athletes, discrimination against their countrymen receded.

Assimilation

Few first-generation Irish Americans made it out of the slums, but many parents sacrificed everything to educate their children and give them the skills they would need to become successful and escape poverty. Children grew up fast in the slums. So many Irish immigrant males died in their late thirties or early forties that it was a rare family that still had a father when the oldest children reached their teen years. Youngsters aged five or six peddled papers or ran errands to earn a little money before going to school. Boys of twelve or thirteen often had to take on full-time jobs to help their families survive. But they did survive. By the early part of the twentieth century, many Irish Americans found themselves edging into the middle class. And the future looked bright and hopeful.

In the late twentieth century, Irish Americans have been so thoroughly assimilated into the general U.S. population that many think of themselves as simply American. Second-, third-, and fourth-generation Irish Americans have contributed substantially to American society, and they have adopted the lifestyle and values of this country. The election of John Fitzgerald Kennedy to the presidency in 1960 proved once and for all that Catholic Irish Americans were accepted as being "as American as anyone else."

Feeling comfortable about their status in America, Irish Americans have recently put effort into rediscovering their Irish roots.

Like New York Representative Hugh Carey (shown in 1962 with his family), many descendants of Irish immigrants have found success as they assimilated into U.S. society.

They have taken new pride in reviving old customs and attempting to trace their family histories. The result has given a new meaning to being Irish American.

FITTING IN

Some Irish immigrants were so anxious to become a part of American society that they were willing to do almost anything. Many changed their names: O'Connor became Connor, and O'Brien could become Bryant. Some changed their faith, becoming Protestants. Ambitious Irish immigrants eagerly learned to speak without a brogue and to use standard grammar. Few, though, went as far as an Irish American named Fleming.

In 1909, when he was twenty-one years old, Fleming walked into a dentist's office in Jersey City and told the dentist to pull out all of his teeth. He then bought a set of good false teeth. He believed his crooked teeth marked him as a lower-class Irishman and that having them "corrected" would further his political ambitions. His ploy seemed to work. During his career, Mr. Fleming was elected to many local political offices.

A girl wears a "tattoo" of the Irish flag at an Irish American festival. Loyalty to family and community in America is often linked to the pride Irish Americans take in tracing their family roots to Ireland.

CHAPTER THREE

FAMILY AND COMMUNITY
THE IRISH AMERICAN FAMILY

When Tim Russert, a news analyst, was growing up in a mostly Irish American neighborhood in south Buffalo, New York, a neighbor boy objected to the "Kennedy for President" sign on his front lawn. The neighbor boy slugged Russert. Russert says, "I went back with one of my sisters and we sat on him." The neighbor boy should have realized two things about Irish Americans: They don't tolerate insult, and their families stick together.

An Intense Family Loyalty

For the majority of Irish Americans, the family is one of their most important priorities. Though some have a hard time saying what they feel, there is no question about where their loyalty lies. The intense bond that most Irish Americans feel, not just for their immediate family members, but also for their entire extended family, can probably be traced back to their Celtic roots.

The Celtic people settled in Ireland about 300 B.C. Theirs was a tribal society without any centralized authority. The people gave their loyalty to their clan, instead of to a monarch or to their country. The clans frequently quarreled with one another, which is one reason the British conquered them so easily. The British, after they conquered Ireland, tried to impose a centralized government on the Irish people. But that government proved to be so oppressive and corrupt,

it did not tempt the Irish people to shift their loyalty. Instead, they gave their allegiance to their family, friends, and neighbors.

This pattern did not change when Irish immigrants settled in the United States. Irish immigrants were not welcome outside the communities they built in the city slums. Within those communities and the ones they built later in the suburbs, Irish Americans built a complex system of social, educational, and spiritual relationships, and the center of those relationships was the family.

The Family Unit

The Irish American family is often matriarchal. In early immigrant days, this was a necessity. Irish American males frequently died in their thirties or forties, usually from overwork. The widow pulled the family together and kept it going.

In modern times, Irish American women are rarely submissive wives. In fact, an Irish American woman often achieves what one writer described as "a happy equality in her relationship with her husband." Irish American women take a leading role in family decision-making and are often almost solely responsible for disciplining the children. A 1980s survey found that most Irish American children reported themselves as feeling closer to their mothers than to their fathers and more likely to talk to their mothers than to their fathers.

THE RIGHTS OF WOMEN

Historically, the Irish have always granted women a lot of power. In ancient Celtic times, women were not given equal rights with men, but they did have more of a voice in decision-making than women in most other ancient societies. In the Middle Ages through the Victorian age, women could choose to enter a convent rather than marry. Though some may not see this as much of a choice, it was more of a career choice than most women had then, and many women found (and find) considerable challenge and satisfaction in a nun's life.

Irish American men are seemingly comfortable with powerful women. They are just as likely as women to support feminist issues, and they adopt a liberal stand on appropriate roles for women. In fact, the only demographic category of Irish American Catholics to show a majority in favor of women as priests is males over the age of forty-five.

There are many stories about Irish American mothers forcing their sons into the priesthood to satisfy their own selfish pride or playing the self-sacrificing martyr's role to keep their children tied to them. Some Irish American mothers have abused the power and influence they exert over their children, but many Irish American women have combined their authority with tenderness and affection, and their strength has sustained

Mother and daughter take delight in each other's company at an Irish festival in suburban New Jersey. Irish American mothers are a source of love, compassion, and authority in their families.

their families through difficult times and spurred their children on to achievement. The typical Irish American mother is willing to work very hard to see that her children have every advantage and opportunity possible.

The Irish American father is often less prominent in family life, but not less important. Though he may not challenge his wife's role in the family, he is an authority to be respected and obeyed by his children. Occasionally some Irish American husbands and fathers conform to the old stereotype of the irresponsible drunken Irishman. However, most are conscientious and hard working, taking seriously the responsibility of supporting their families. Irish American author Mary Higgins Clark has recalled the days when her father, trying to keep the family business afloat, put in twenty-hour work days. And Irish American journalist Bernard McCormick remembered the self-discipline and goodness of his father and recorded that he was "simply the best man I knew."

Expressing Affection

Irish Americans, like any other group of people, have had problems within their family structure. One of the most often discussed is the difficulty they seem to have expressing emotions, especially love. This seems to date back to the time of the potato famine, when so many families were destroyed or separated by starvation and emigration. Author Andrew M. Greeley tells the story of an old woman who sat at the side of her husband's deathbed. "Shamus," the old woman said, "never once in all the fifty years that we have been married have you ever said you love me."

"Ooch, woman," her husband replied, "surely there was no need of that. You knew it all along, didn't ya?"

LOTS AND LOTS OF CHILDREN

There is a stereotype of Irish American families as unquestioningly following the Pope's edict not to use birth control and thus producing lots and lots of children. In fact, most Irish American families disagree with and disregard the Catholic Church's prohibition of birth control. Nevertheless, they do tend to want and to have larger families than the U.S. population in general. Sociologist Andrew Greeley attributes this to the simple fact that Irish Americans like babies.

The Irish seem to have pulled back from expressing such emotion as a way of protecting themselves from loss. This does not mean that they feel emotion any less strongly than other people. Irish American novelist Thomas Fleming recalled that in his rebellious teenage years, he once accused his tough, autocratic father of not caring about him or his brother. They were in the car at the time.

His father ran the car off the road and leaped out of the car, crying. As Fleming fearfully approached, his father, who was striding up and down the side of the road, sobbed, "You said I didn't love you. . . . You and your brother. You're all I've got." The intensity is there. But it is rarely allowed out.

Siblings

The bond Irish American families feel for one another is often especially strong between siblings, though there may also be intense competitiveness as well. An older brother may pick on a younger one and fight with him all the time. Yet if that brother gets in trouble, he is there instantly, ready to help. Adult siblings may not like each other, may not share common interests, and may find each other boring, but most would never miss getting together for holidays, birthdays, and

other special occasions. Whatever may happen within the family, to outsiders, they present a united front.

Patterns of Communication

The Irish have always been a sociable people. An old Irish proverb says that even fighting is better than loneliness. Surveys have shown that Irish Americans tend to talk more than most other people, more than fifteen hours a week to their spouses and more than seventeen hours a week to their children. Irish and Irish Americans have a reputation as hard drinkers, but in fact, they don't drink any more than the average American. They just prefer to do it at a pub with their friends where it is more noticeable than in their homes.

Most Irish Americans prefer to conduct business through conversation. They are

A New York Irish pub invites patrons to view the '94 Ireland-Norway World Cup soccer match. Irish Americans are known for their hospitality, gift of conversation, and affection for fellow humans.

A recent arrival in New York from Ireland is fitted for her wedding dress. Because being married once meant bringing children into a world filled with hunger, poverty, and political or ethnic oppression, many Irish couples used to put off marriage until they were older.

impatient with bureaucracy and red tape. If something needs to be taken care of, they prefer informal lines of communication, a simple chat with the person in power rather than memos and committee meetings.

Delayed Marriages

Prior to the potato famine, Irish peasants often married as teenagers. There was no reason to wait, as they knew they would never own much of anything. Their family would divide the land they lived on, and the village would help them throw up a mud cottage. But the devastation of the famine changed this outlook.

In the years following the potato famine, the Irish began delaying their marriages until they had some sort of economic security. They worried about bringing children that they could not feed into the world, and they were aware that overpopulation had contributed to the effects of the famine. They often delayed marriage for years, and sometimes never married at all.

Irish immigrants for several generations continued to wait years before they married. Andrew Greeley tells us that in the early part of this century, his parents, aunts, and uncles all waited until they were in their early thirties to marry. Mary Higgins Clark reports that her parents "courted" for seven years and were nearly forty when they married. The post-World War II generations changed to an age closer to the American norm. But even today, there is a slight difference in when Irish Americans marry. The average Irish American male marries at 24.5 years; the average Irish American female at 22 years, both a little more than a year later than the average for most other Americans.

Family Goals

In most Irish American marriages, security is an important issue. Irish American families often seek some security in their lives in two ways: by buying a house and by gaining "respectability."

Under the British penal laws, Irish Catholics were not permitted to own land. Even after those laws were repealed, few Irish peasants could afford to buy even a small plot of land. This left them at the mercy of landlords and gave them no resources when the famine struck. Poor, starving Irish immigrants saw in America the chance of owning their own home as the opportunity for some security in their lives. Few Irish potato famine immigrants achieved that goal, but their children and grandchildren did. One Irish American woman recorded that when her parents were finally able to buy a six-room, brick house in the Bronx, her mother regarded it as "Buckingham Palace, the Taj Mahal, and Shangri-La" all wrapped up in one.

Along with a house, Irish Americans have sought "respectability." Under British rule and as despised "foreigners" in the United States, the Irish have been labeled as inferior and treated as second-class citizens. As Irish immigrants made a place for themselves in the United States, they have sought acceptance from the majority.

This 1934 photo of the Kennedy family shows John and Robert in the back row and Edward (Ted) held by his father in the front. Despite the success and political power that would become a Kennedy trademark, family members felt the sting of prejudice against Irish Catholics all their lives.

Many Irish Americans attempt to become more "American" than other Americans. These Irish Americans are intensely patriotic, and many have distinguished themselves in the U.S. armed services. However, some Irish Americans, hoping to be accepted, have chosen to slavishly copy the lifestyle and values of the upper class — at least as they perceive it. To them, appearance is of the utmost importance. They must live in the right kind of house, wear the right kind of clothes, drive the right kind of car, and go to the right kind of school. The most important question is, "What will people say?" Sometimes appearance is more important than reality. One can cope with a child causing trouble in school or a husband drinking too much — unless the neighbors find out. These Irish Americans live with a terrible fear of being rejected.

Even some of the very richest Irish Americans still feel insecure about their place in society — and with some justification. Some of the "best" clubs and social organizations still discriminate against Catholics. Stephen Birmingham tells the story of how John F. Kennedy, while a student at Harvard, once brought home a classmate who was from one of Boston's most prominent families. Rose Kennedy, J. F. K.'s mother, became nervous and tense in front of this young man, and finally asked him, "Tell me, when are the nice

These women enjoy the music, good fun, and camaraderie at an Irish American fair.

people of Boston going to accept us?" Despite all the power, prestige, and wealth of the Kennedy family, she still felt second class.

Irish Americans whose families settled in the Midwest and West seem less affected by this deep insecurity. Society is looser and more flexible in those regions than on the East Coast, and Irish Americans found it easier to establish themselves. But even today, sociologists have noted that Irish American youth often have less self-confidence than those of some other ethnic groups.

"Who do they think they are?"

Though many Irish Americans cherish their position in middle- and upper-class society, they are quick to ridicule those of their own who "give themselves airs." In early immigrant society, most Irish Americans were "shanty Irish," living in tarpaper shacks or dank slum cellars. Shanty Irish were proud of being Irish and refused to compromise that pride. However, some Irish Americans shifted their allegiance, foregoing loyalty to their fellow immigrants in order to get ahead in the mainstream culture. Occasionally these Irish Americans became rich. They then became known as "lace curtain" Irish. Eventually that nickname came to have more positive associations. Lace curtain Irish were those who had raised themselves out of the slums and into affluence. But a segment of Irish Americans still proudly call themselves "shanty Irish," and they disparage the pretensions of those who think they have risen above their roots. Their nickname for them: T. T. Irish — "two-toilet Irish."

Neighborhoods

Whether shanty Irish or T. T. Irish, suburbanite or city dweller, Irish Americans have usually sought to live near each other. Though poverty and discrimination originally forced them into particular areas, they would probably have chosen to stick together even if they'd had a choice, as later generations have shown. For wherever Irish Americans settle, they don't simply live next door to one another — they become neighbors.

For many Irish Americans, the neighborhood is their extended family. And until recently, it was likely that it would contain many aunts, uncles, and grandparents. Bernard McCormick says that at one time his mother had twenty relatives living on the same street.

Irish American neighborhoods were like small villages within big cities. Children roamed about freely, without fear. There was always some sort of game, softball or football, at the local park. There were smells of baking and clean laundry and incense from the church. Men gathered in the local pub to talk politics and sports. Women gathered on street corners and exchanged gossip. Everybody knew everybody — and everybody else's business.

There used to be hundreds of these neighborhoods, scattered throughout the cities of the United States. Many have disappeared. As Irish Americans moved up economically, they tended to move out of the old neighborhoods. In New Orleans, the section of the city originally settled by Irish famine immigrants

A HOUSE IS TO BE LIVED IN

Though many Irish Americans care about appearances, and they love their homes, housework does not seem to be a high priority for Irish American women or men. In a survey of college-graduate women, Irish Americans came in last of all ethnic groups both rating themselves as housekeepers and rating the satisfaction they get from housekeeping. Father Andrew Greeley reports that his mother was made a nervous wreck by a neighbor woman of Polish descent because that woman's house was always immaculate, with not an item out of place. Mrs. Greeley may have been intimidated by such perfection, but, Irish to the core, she didn't change her own priorities. "A house is meant to live in, not to admire," she said. Journalist Bernard McCormick recalls that his father did the housework in their home because his mother hated it so much. Today, in both the workplace and in the home, the Irish are unlikely to be obsessive about neatness; but then, as they see it, they have more important things to do.

Bainbridge, a neighborhood in the Bronx, New York, has long been home to Irish American families and businesses. Many urban neighborhoods still retain the flavor and culture of Irish America.

is known as the Irish Channel. But the only Irish Americans still living there are nuns ministering to the poor. Other cities have seen the same.

But not all the neighborhoods are gone. A section of Springfield, Massachusetts, known as Hungry Hill is as vital and alive an Irish neighborhood as ever. The neighbors meet at the John Boyle O'Reilly club after mass on Sundays and talk of politics and events in the neighborhood. Someone always has the latest sports scores from Ireland. Jokes are exchanged and drinks are downed. Gaelic words sprinkle the conversation. The number of Irish Americans in Hungry Hill has declined since the days the *City Directory* listed six hundred Sullivans and two hundred O'Briens, but the spirit is still fiercely Irish.

There does seem to be hope for the survival of such neighborhoods. Younger Irish Americans don't automatically move away any more. They like the convenience of the location and they enjoy the atmosphere of these neighborhoods. Many are buying the old houses and restoring them, and in so doing they are bringing to life the classic Irish American neighborhood once more.

The Future

The status of the Irish American neighborhoods can almost be said to be the status of distinctly Irish American families. There are many who say Irish Americans have assimilated so completely into the mainstream American culture that they really aren't a distinct ethnic group any more. Yet just as there are still thriving Irish American neighborhoods, there are still many thriving Irish American families. They are proud of their heritage and certain that their unique culture has something of value to offer to the United States. Family loyalty and family traditions bind Irish American families together as tightly as ever.

Bagpipers march past St. Patrick's Cathedral in New York's St. Patrick's Day Parade. The Catholic Church has been an inseparable part of life for most Irish people since the fifth century.

CHAPTER FOUR

RELIGION AND CELEBRATIONS
IRISH AMERICA AND THE CATHOLIC CHURCH

In 1901, a young Irish American graduated from the eighth grade. His pastor called him into the rectory to ask him his plans for the future. The young boy confided his dream of becoming a professional baseball player. The priest responded, "No, you're not. We've got enough tramp Irish athletes. I've watched you play. You're a good fielder, but you can't hit a curve. You're going to business school." There was no debate. The young man accepted the priest's edict and spent the next year in business school.

From the time the Irish famine immigrants arrived in the United States through most of the twentieth century, the center of the Irish community in America was the Catholic Church, and the person with the most honor and authority was the Catholic priest. Especially in the late nineteenth century, Irish immigrants in the U.S. found themselves in poverty-stricken, alien surroundings, confronted by a hostile population. The only familiar thing in this new life was the church, and they clung to it as to a lifeline.

Roots in the Old Country

The Irish people had always been a devout people. St. Patrick introduced Christianity to Ireland in the fifth century, and within fifteen years after his arrival, nearly every person in Ireland had eagerly embraced this new religion. During the Middle Ages and up to the birth of Protestantism in the sixteenth century, Irish monks were renowned throughout Europe for their scholarship.

The Catholic Church in Ireland was largely unaffected by Protestantism until 1534, when King Henry VIII of England broke with the Catholic Church and tried to force Ireland to do likewise. When the Irish people refused to give up Catholicism, King Henry and his successors passed the infamous Penal Laws (see Chapter One). Some Irish Catholics, especially Irish aristocracy, converted to Protestantism in order to get an education, which the Penal Laws denied to Catholics, or to keep their land. But the intense persecution caused the majority of the Irish people simply to become more devoted than ever to the Catholic faith. And the cause of Irish independence became linked to the Catholic Church.

In most European countries, the Catholic Church was a wealthy church tied to great political power, but in Ireland, Catholicism was outlawed for generations. Its priests were not powerful authority figures, but victims. Priests lived in poverty and risked their lives to say mass and educate Irish children. In turn, the people endangered themselves to shelter the priests. This led to a relationship of mutual loyalty and trust between priest and parishioner that was unlike that found outside Ireland. Throughout the centuries of English oppression, the Catholic Church became the one institution in which the Irish could have faith.

The Irish Immigrant Church

When the Irish immigrants settled in North America, they chose areas where Irish communities were already established, such as New York City, Boston, and New Orleans. Wherever they settled, building a church was their first priority. The Irish had never had government support for building their churches, as other Catholic countries had, so they didn't expect it now. Irish immigrants might work a fifteen-hour day for fifty cents, but they saved their pennies for the building fund, and everyone in the community took great pride in a beautiful church. The Irish people took even greater pride in encouraging their best and brightest children to become priests and nuns.

The Catholic Church provided Irish immigrants with much more than spiritual comfort. The parish church was the center of all social, political, educational, and religious activities. The church held dances and political rallies. It sponsored athletic teams. The

ST. PATRICK

Magonus Succatus Patricius, better known as St. Patrick, is the patron saint of Ireland and beloved in America as well. Patrick lived in the fifth century. He was the son of a wealthy, but not very religious, family in England. When Patrick was almost sixteen years old, raiders from Ireland attacked England. They kidnapped Patrick and others as slaves. Patrick was taken to Ireland, where he lived for six years in bondage, tending pigs, sheep, and cattle. As a boy, he had never spent much time praying, but he began doing so now. One night, he had a vision, which he believed was from God, telling him to escape. He ran away and eventually made his way back to England, where he trained as a priest. When the Church needed someone to go to Ireland to preach the gospel, he offered to go. Harboring no bitterness or anger toward those who had kidnapped and enslaved him, Patrick preached of the love of God. The Irish people accepted these ideas and converted by the thousands. Within St. Patrick's lifetime, nearly every person in Ireland converted to Christianity.

Inside St. Patrick's Cathedral in New York. Irish Americans have long played a dominant role in the Catholic Church in America.

people looked to the church as a place to socialize with their neighbors and appealed to the priests to help settle their problems. The Catholic Church gave Irish immigrants a sense of value and dignity denied them by the general population.

In the years following immigration, Irish Catholics centered their lives around their parishes. When asked where they lived, Irish Catholics usually responded with the name of their parish instead of the street or section of town. In the days of "No Irish Need Apply," the church provided a place where Irish Americans were not just accepted; they were eagerly welcomed.

THE LEGEND OF THE SHAMROCK

The shamrock is the national flower of Ireland and an internationally recognized symbol of the Emerald Isle. Legend states that the shamrock became special to the Irish in the fifth century. St. Patrick was having difficulty explaining the doctrine of the trinity to the Irish people. He bent down and plucked a shamrock from the ground and showed it to the people. The shamrock has three leaves and yet is one plant. So, too, he explained, God is Father, Son, and Holy Spirit, and yet one God. From that day to this, the shamrock has been considered good luck.

A group of students from a Catholic school in suburban Chicago. Many parents believe that parochial schools give children the right mix of learning, religious training, and discipline.

Parochial Schools

Irish Catholics in the United States were not prevented from attending public schools, but they were not particularly welcome there. The public school curriculum in the late nineteenth century presented a strict Anglo-Saxon view of the world, a view that dismissed the Irish and their culture as inferior and unimportant. But the Irish had dealt with this situation before. In Ireland, priests had run hedge schools; now they and nuns and monks opened parochial schools for their children. Though these schools separated Irish American children from the mainstream culture, they provided a supportive atmosphere in which these children were expected and helped to succeed.

At first, the parochial schools were not very good. There wasn't much money, and the teachers were more dedicated than qualified. But parents were determined that the schools should succeed and provided both economic and moral support. The schools had two goals: to give Irish Catholic children the basic skills (reading, writing, and arithmetic) they needed to obtain middle-class jobs and to teach those children the fundamentals of the Catholic faith.

As time passed, the schools improved. Catholic schools flourished across the nation and gained the respect and admiration of the general population. Today, many parents from a wide variety of racial, religious, and ethnic backgrounds place their children in Catholic schools, where they feel the children will get a better education than the public schools can provide. The Catholic Church has also opened many colleges and universities, including some of the finest in the country, such as Notre Dame and Georgetown University.

Social Services

Irish Catholic churches in America have also always been concerned about caring for the physical needs of their parishioners. During the latter half of the nineteenth century, they started many hospitals, orphanages, and almshouses for the poor. Irish Catholic nuns serving as teachers and principals, nurses, and hospital administrators were among the first women in this country to be given the opportunity to succeed professionally. Public admiration for their work and for the fine schools and hospitals they ran did a lot to help reduce the prejudice against Catholics.

Volunteers meet at a community center for Irish immigrants in the Bronx, New York, to prepare food for donation.

IRISH AND PROTESTANT

Of course, not all of the Irish who immigrated to the United States were Catholic. Though Protestants were a minority, there were still significant numbers of Irish Protestants who made the long journey. Their story is different than that of Irish Catholics, but they, too, had a significant impact on American culture.

Irish Protestants tended to enter the United States through Philadelphia and then often moved into the South. They began calling themselves Scotch Irish after Irish Catholics began coming in large numbers, because they wished to emphasize the difference between themselves and those "shanty Irish." Their ancestors were Scottish citizens whom Queen Elizabeth I had encouraged to settle in Northern Ireland as she tried to replace Catholic Irish citizens there with Protestants who were loyal to England.

Scotch Irish tended to be hard working, serious citizens. Unlike the famine Irish immigrants, many of them chose to become farmers or head west to the frontier. Few of these Irish were discriminated against as were Irish Catholics. Because they were of Anglo-Saxon stock and of the Protestant faith, they had a much easier time fitting into the majority culture in the United States.

Once a week, these volunteer Irish Catholic workers distribute food and a hot cup of coffee to homeless people.

The Other Catholics

Of course, the Irish were not the only Catholics in the United States. In the later half of the nineteenth century, many of the immigrants from Germany, France, Italy, and Eastern European countries were also Catholic. But the Irish immigrants had gotten here first. They were the first large group of Catholics to enter this country, and they were particularly assertive in preserving and promoting their beliefs.

The Irish dominated the Catholic Church throughout the nineteenth century and into the twentieth, forming a church that met the needs of its people. They created a church with a strong focus on providing social services, community activities, and quality education, along with an ardent allegiance to the Pope.

Irish domination of the American Catholic Church was so evident that in the 1880s some German Catholics rebelled. They proposed a restructuring of the Church by nationality. Church districts would be formed by ethnic background rather than by geographic location. Irish American Catholic leaders appealed to the Pope, who rejected the German Catholic proposal. The Irish retained their leadership in the American Catholic Church and never relinquished it. Even into the 1990s, the Irish influence is apparent in the Catholic Church in America. While only about 18 percent of the sixty million Catholics in the United States today claim Irish ancestry, almost 50 percent of the priests and nuns are Irish American. Many of these are first-generation Irish immigrants from such schools as the Missionary College of All Hallows in Dublin, which has sent nearly fourteen hundred priests to the United States.

The Middle Class and the Catholic Church

The Catholic Church and parish activities continued to be an important part of Irish Americans' lives into the twentieth century, after many of them entered the middle class and moved to the suburbs. Many second- and third-generation Irish Americans actively sought a parish in the suburbs that could provide their children with the atmosphere of love and acceptance that had been so important to their own parents when they were growing up in their own city parish.

AN IRISH PRAYER

May those that love us, love us.
And those that don't love us,
May God turn their hearts.
And if He doesn't turn their hearts,
May He turn their ankles,
So we'll know them by their limping!

But in the 1960s, the relationship between the Irish American Catholics and their church began to change. With the election of John F. Kennedy to the White House, most Irish Americans finally felt completely accepted as part of American society. Though

An Irish volunteer (center) poses with an Irish American nun and priest after distributing food to homeless people. Irish Catholic clergy have long looked after the needs of others.

anti-Catholic rhetoric emerged during Kennedy's campaign, it was rejected by the majority of Americans. Irish Americans no longer needed their church to be a sanctuary apart from the mainstream culture. They were now welcome at the country club and the Rotary meetings. But this success did not cause them to turn their back on their church. In fact, quite the opposite happened. Irish Americans filled the churches, and idealistic young people flocked into seminaries and convents.

Filled with a new confidence, Irish Americans expected the Church to reflect their new vision. But problems emerged.

Dissent

The American tradition has always allowed for dissent and public discussion of policy. But the Roman Catholic Church expects obedience to its authority. Edicts handed down by the Pope are not subject to debate. Many Irish Americans disagreed with the official positions taken by Rome forbidding clergy marriage, birth control, divorce, abortion, and ordaining women as priests. They expected Rome to be willing to reconsider its position on those and other social issues, but Rome was not. The changes made after the Second Vatican Council (1962-1965), such as changing the mass from Latin to English and using modern music, were not what newly vocal American Catholics were seeking. Many judged these changes as superficial, and others felt they removed the mystery and meaning from worship.

For the first time in history, Irish Americans began to leave the Catholic Church in significant numbers. Over the next twenty years, financial contributions dropped, and a large number of convents, schools, and churches had to be closed. Respect for the priesthood and sisterhood diminished. No longer were the best and brightest Irish American young people encouraged to become priests or nuns. They were now channeled into careers in business and industry and the various professions. (Some of this change can be attributed to the fact that some of those career choices had not been available previously, especially to women.) In 1964, there were about 45,000 men preparing for the priesthood. By 1984, this number dropped to about 12,000, the decline due in large part to fewer Irish Americans choosing the priesthood as a career. In 1965, there were more than 181,000 nuns in the United States. Fifteen years later, this number was reduced by more than 50,000.

The 1990s

Despite these problems, a large number of Irish Americans today are as devoted as ever to their Church. Though not as submissive as their ancestors, they still claim the Catholic Church as their own and turn to it for spiritual strength and instruction. Even those who rarely attend mass consider themselves Catholic and usually arrange to have their children baptized and confirmed. Their Church has also made an effort to regain its congregation. Historic St. Patrick's Church in Chicago, the oldest public building to survive the Chicago Fire in 1871, listed just four members in 1983, and there was talk of turning it into a museum. But through the dedication and hard work of a small group of Irish American Catholics, St. Patrick's survived and rebuilt its congregation. At the close of 1993, that parish could claim a vital and thriving congregation of fifteen hundred registered members and over twelve thousand associates. Other churches have done the same. The Irish Americans and the Catholic Church still have some issues to resolve, but they are working on it.

The Sacraments

Though the Catholic Church is no longer the only institution to which Irish Americans turn for social, spiritual, and educational activities, it still plays a major role in the lives of many Irish Americans, especially children. Many Irish American families set up statues of Mary, the mother of Jesus, in their homes. Children may decorate these shrines with flowers, and some families hold nightly prayers near them.

There are also a number of very important occasions celebrated with special ceremonies in the church. The first is baptism. Babies are presented to God in a special ceremony during or just after mass, usually within a few weeks of their birth. Often the infants wear special long white gowns, representing purity, which may have been worn by babies in their family for generations. The priest pours holy (blessed) water over the baby's head in front of the congregation, and their souls, washed clean, are dedicated to God. The infants are anointed with holy oil on the breast with the sign of the cross, between the shoulders, and on the head, and salt, a symbol of immortality, may be placed on their tongue. Godparents stand up with the children, promising to be sure that the children are instructed in spiritual matters. A lighted candle may be given to the one baptized to remind the child to "Remember those early days when the light first came to

This missal, which contains songs and prayers that make up the order of the mass, sits on a pew at St. Patrick's Cathedral in New York, a spiritual focal point for most Irish Catholics in America.

Following a period of intense instruction in the teachings and rites of the Catholic faith comes a special time in the lives of young Irish Catholics: receiving their First Communion.

to the front of the church during a special mass. A hymn may be sung and prayers said, and questions and answers about the Catholic faith are recited. Then the priest gives each child a piece of bread and a sip of wine to remember the Last Supper of Jesus before his crucifixion. After First Communion, most families hold a big party to celebrate. A traditional gift for girls on this occasion is a gold cross on a chain. Prayer books and rosary beads may be given to both boys and girls.

A serious occasion is the sacrament of penance or confession, which usually takes place about a year before First Communion. Children are taught that inappropriate behavior has consequences, but that God can forgive them for the things they do wrong if they confess their sins. Children speak to the priest, one at a time, in privacy, confessing the things they have done wrong. The priest will usually advise them to say prayers or do a specific action, called penance, to make up for their mistakes. Then he assures them that they are forgiven. Catholics are encouraged to make their confession at least once a year thereafter, usually during Lent.

you." (Hebrews 10:32) That candle is often kept and lit again on the anniversary of the baptism and on other special occasions.

When children reach six or seven, they begin catechism classes. In many churches, children attend a class once a week for two years, to be instructed in their faith. At the end of that time, they receive their First Communion. This is a special and important occasion. Girls wear white dresses, often like short wedding gowns, and sometimes even including a veil. Boys wear suits. They walk

In junior high or high school, Catholic youth decide if they wish to "confirm" the promises made for them at their baptism. This again takes place during a special ceremony called Confirmation. During this rite, the youths answer questions about the Catholic faith. They usually kneel before the bishop, who anoints their foreheads with oil in the sign of the cross. The youths may take sponsors who can help them grow spiritually and may add another name to the names given at baptism.

The Catholic Church also has special ceremonies for weddings. An Irish American wedding is celebrated with great joy. The beautiful church ceremony is usually followed by a reception, often characterized by much singing and socializing.

The Sacrament of the Sick, given to those who may be dying, allows a seriously ill person to ask for healing and a dying person to confess his or her sins and enter heaven in a state of grace.

The Future

Irish Americans have been described as being "Catholic like no one else." They have a long rich history in that Church. The Catholic Church gave Irish immigrants security and hope. It provided them with the social services, education, and sense of iden-

AN IRISH BLESSING

May the road rise to meet you.
May the wind be always at your back.
May the sun shine warm upon your face,
And the rain fall soft upon your fields.
And until we meet again,
May God hold you in the hollow of His hand.

tity Irish immigrants needed to raise themselves out of poverty. In the twentieth century, the Catholic Church has provided many Irish Americans with meaning and purpose in their lives. Though the relationship between Irish Americans and their church is changing, they will enter the twenty-first century together.

Marriage is a sacrament of the Catholic Church and is a time when Irish Catholics both celebrate the joining of two lives and reaffirm their relationship with the Church.

The Irish have long had a special talent for many kinds of artistic expression. For these youngsters, a gathering of Irish Americans has produced a burst of energy in the form of a dance.

CHAPTER FIVE

CUSTOMS, EXPRESSIONS, AND HOSPITALITY
CULTURE AND TRADITIONS

Irish American author Mary Higgins Clark tells of the struggle her family went through after her father died in 1939. Her mother tried to find a job, but didn't succeed. Eventually they ended up taking boarders into their home, but even so, they barely managed to make ends meet. One morning, just before dawn, a boarder who had fallen behind in his rent tried to sneak out. He tripped over a lamp and roused the family. Ms. Clark's mother confronted him: "If you didn't have the money, you should have told me. God knows, I can understand that." The man left with two dollars in his hand.

Hospitality

The Irish are famous for their tradition of hospitality. In Ireland, hospitality was a way of life, practiced by everyone. People shared what little they had and helped one another in time of need. Even at the height of the potato famine, no stranger would be turned away without being offered a bit of whatever food was available. Throughout the years, the friendly courtesy and generous open-handedness of the Irish people have impressed visitors from every corner of the earth.

When the Irish came to America, they soon learned that no such tradition existed

These Irish musicians play weekly at an Irish pub in New York City. The group uses electrified instruments and combines traditional Irish music with other influences to create a modern sound.

here, at least not toward Irish immigrants. A different attitude — individualism — prevailed. The aggressive, me-first type was the one who succeeded. Someone who hoarded food didn't die of starvation. And the people who stole from others simply improved their own lifestyles.

In the Irish villages, people who were selfish or rude were ridiculed and ostracized. No such control existed in America. There was even a certain admiration among Americans for ruthlessness. Most Irish immigrants did not lose their attitude of hospitality, as Ms. Clark's mother amply illustrates, but they often learned to confine it to taking care of their own.

This Celtic cross is surrounded by flowers at a festival in the Midwest. Many Irish Americans have worked to keep ancient Irish culture alive.

Clannishness

The Irish have often been accused of clannishness, but their loyalty to one another was frequently a matter of survival. The American-born population of the United States often turned their backs on the Irish, so they stuck together, fiercely and proudly. If one of them found a job, he or she tried to get other Irish immigrants taken on at the same place. If some of their own were competing in sporting events, they cheered for them; and if there was an Irish name on the ballot, they were sure to check that box.

Today, Irish Americans are still loyal to one another, though no longer exclusively so. Still, Irish American newspapers, such as the *Irish American Post* or the *Irish American News*, are filled with endorsements of Irish American politicians before an election. It is no longer necessity that makes Irish Americans stick together, but a new-found pride in their heritage.

Celtic People

While the British ruled in Ireland, they ruthlessly suppressed the native Celtic culture. They banned the Gaelic language, forbade the practice of Catholicism, and belittled the Irish traditions of scholarship and art. During the centuries of British rule, many Irish traditions and ideas were lost. Stories telling of Celtic heroes and Celtic custom were passed from parent to child, but as poverty and disease took their toll, many of these stories and customs did not survive. Added to this was the weight of British scorn. As generation after generation was told its culture had never produced anything worthwhile, the Irish began to believe it and so did not try to preserve their own culture.

As Irish Americans sought acceptance in the United States, many felt that improving the status of Ireland would improve the status of the Irish in America. For some, this meant working to free Ireland from British rule. And indeed, both the weight of world public opinion stirred up by Irish Americans and the dollars they donated to the Irish nationalist cause were instrumental in the formation of the Irish Free State in 1921. But others turned their attention to reviving the Celtic culture. They researched the documents that had survived and used archeology and interviews to add to their knowledge. They rediscovered a rich and fascinating world.

A Land of Poets

To no one's surprise, the Celtic culture has proved to have a rich tradition of literary excellence. From *The Book of Kells* to the brilliance of James Joyce, the Irish have produced what one writer has claimed to be

> ## THE BOOK OF KELLS
>
> One of the treasures of Ireland is *The Book of Kells*. This illuminated manuscript was completed by monks at the monastery of Kells in County Meath, Ireland, in the eighth century. *The Book of Kells* includes a version of the Gospels from the New Testament of the Bible and accounts of Irish history. Its pages contain elaborate ornamentation and exquisite illustrations characteristic of Celtic art. It is considered a masterpiece of medieval literature and art. Currently, *The Book of Kells* is in the library at Trinity College in Dublin, Ireland.

"more novelists, poets, storytellers, and playwrights per capita than any other country in the world." The Irish and Irish Americans have discovered a wealth of Celtic myths and

A modern storyteller holds the attention of his young audience at an Irish American festival. The Irish love of life, literature, and spinning tales has endured in Irish America today.

BLARNEY

The Irish have always revered wit and skillful speaking. Among the most adept speakers was Cormac Carthy, the Lord of Blarney. In the sixteenth century Queen Elizabeth I of England tried to force the Irish aristocracy to give up their ownership of their homes and land in Ireland. Those who did so would then receive their lands back as grants from the crown of England. This policy was intended to establish that the English, not the Irish, controlled the ownership of Irish lands. Carthy came to London and pretended to agree, but talked around and around the subject, using "fair words and soft speech" to avoid saying anything to the point. Queen Elizabeth I finally said with exasperation, "This is all Blarney. What he says he never means." The word *blarney* thus entered the English language, meaning skillful flattery or nonsensical speech. And people still travel to Blarney Castle near Cork in Ireland to kiss the Blarney Stone. This action, says tradition, will then grant eloquence to that person.

stories. Tales describing the daring deeds of ancient heroes, such as King Arthur, Finn MacCool, and Cuchulain, celebrate the Celtic warrior and king. Many stories sparkle with wit and humor as they poke fun at people's pretensions. There are tales of love and tales of adventure. And, of course, there are fanciful yarns of leprechauns, fairies, and elves.

Much of the history and legend of the Celtic people has been passed down from generation to generation orally. The bard who told stories and sang songs was an honored person wherever he went in Celtic society. Down through the generations, both men and women have excelled at the art of storytelling, and this tradition is preserved today. "One tale brings on another," says an Irish proverb, and that is as true today as ever. Hundreds of years ago, ancient Irish kings brought together minstrels and poets for yearly contests. Today, Irish festivals, held in cities throughout the United States, often hold oratory contests. In addition, many Irish American newspapers, magazines, and civic organizations sponsor storytelling competitions, as

A QUICK COMEBACK

The slippery tongue of the Irish is a source of admiration and annoyance to many who are not Irish. It is reported that Franklin D. Roosevelt once confronted Irish American Jimmy Walker (right), Mayor of New York City.

"Jimmy," asked FDR, "why do the Irish always answer a question with a question?"

"Do we now?" responded Mayor Walker.

well as poetry writing and short story writing contests.

Celtic Art

Celtic art, too, has proved to have amazing complexity and beauty. The ancient Celts fashioned beautiful jewelry and left intricately carved stone monuments. Much of their art was abstract — complicated patterns with figures of plants, insects, reptiles, birds, fish, mammals, or people. There are also interlaced patterns with unbroken lines in knots, spirals, and other formations. The figures they carved or drew were never realistic, because their religion forbade that. Frequently, they showed arms, legs, and hair intertwined in complex configurations. It was not unusual for gods or people to be shown having various animal parts, such as wings or a tail.

These same patterns were used by Irish monks in their illuminated manuscripts, such as *The Book of Kells,* and in the stained glass windows of Irish convents, monasteries, and churches. Modern artists around the world, including Irish Americans, have created their own beautiful designs in the Celtic style. Their work can be seen in museums and cultural centers across the United States — and in some unexpected places, too, such as on the costumes worn by Irish American dance troops.

Dance

Dance has long been a part of the life of the Irish and the Irish American. In Ireland, when the law prohib-

THE CLADDAGH RING

A traditional gift of love that originated in Ireland, but is equally important in the United States, is the Claddagh Ring. This beautiful gold ring was originally designed about four hundred years ago by a master goldsmith named Richard Joyce, who lived in a small fishing village in Ireland called Claddagh. The ring features a crowned heart held by two hands and can be set with precious stones or made of plain gold. The ring is a symbol of love, friendship, and loyalty. If a person wears the ring on the right hand with the crown turned inward, it means his or her heart is free. If it is worn on the right hand with the crown turned outward, it means the person is looking for love. Worn on the left hand, the ring means the person is spoken for. In recent years, the Claddagh Ring has become a popular wedding band for people of a variety of ethnic backgrounds.

The symbols usually found on the Claddagh Ring representing love, loyalty, and friendship have found their way onto this window ornament.

With arms held at their sides and feet raised in kicks, these Irish American dancers perform steps that are both energetic and disciplined. Irish dancing appeals to Americans of many backgrounds.

ited Irish peasants from dancing, they met after dark at the village crossroads for their celebrations. Today their traditional jigs, step dances, and reels are admired throughout the world.

Irish step dancing is an ancestor of today's tap dancing. It is characterized by rapid, intricate steps. Irish dancers combine explosive movement with an incredible, exquisite grace. Often the arms are held still by the dancers' sides while their feet fly.

The first Irish American dance company, the Trinity Dance Company, based in Chicago and Milwaukee, was formed in 1990. Academies, such as Trinity Academy, had been offering Irish dance instruction for a number of years, but their dance competitions were not open to the public, and few people outside the Irish American community were aware of what Irish dance had to offer. The performances of the Trinity Dancers have helped educate people about this elegant art. The Trinity Dancers have toured throughout the United States and Europe and performed in the Ron Howard film *Backdraft*. They have also appeared on a variety of talk shows, including "The Tonight Show," and at the Grand Ole Opry in Nashville. The Trinity Dancers are the only dance company from outside the British Isles ever to win first place in the World Championship of Irish dancing held annually in Ireland — a feat they have accomplished twice.

But Irish dancing isn't limited to professionals. Visit any social gathering of the Irish

American community and you're likely to see someone perform a spirited jig!

Music

Even more popular in the Irish American community is traditional Irish music, both song and instrumental. Mary Higgins Clark recalls her mother and other guests gathering around the piano, singing "Molly Malone" at three in the morning. Journalist/author Pete Hamill records that one of his earliest memories is of his father and friends of his father singing together in the local pub. Professionals, such as Tony Kenny, Phil Coulter, and the Chieftains, perform for capacity crowds. Irish songs include a wide variety of types — ballads, love songs, drinking songs, political songs, and songs of home — but nearly always they are the type of song people want to join in on. At Fifty-seventh Street and

HOPE FOR THE FUTURE

Much of modern dance in America has a dual heritage: Irish and African. This fact was celebrated and enhanced at the August 1993 Milwaukee Irish Fest. The Trinity Dance Company joined with the African American Alyo Children's Dance Theatre of Chicago. Supported by the Celtic rock band Fitz and the Celts and African American drummers, they provided what the *Irish American Post* described as "mind-boggling percussion fervor . . . [in a] vibrant, heart-pounding presentation." The *Post* went on to say, "This is the way life should be. Young people together — dancing, making music, holding hands — whether black, white, brown, yellow . . . or whatever religion, political, or ethnic background."

The Garden State Ceili Band performs at an annual Irish festival in New Jersey. From pubs to fairs and concert halls, Irish music appeals to Americans' love of both the traditional and the modern.

enjoyed throughout the United States.

But not all Irish American music is strictly traditional. Celtic rock bands, such as Fitz and the Celts, the Ghillies, and McTavish, have combined the driving rhythms of rock with the lyricism of Celtic music to produce an exciting and moving sound. Irish bands, such as U2 and the Cinnamons, have exerted a tremendous influence on the contemporary music scene. As a director for MCA records has said, "There's a deep-rooted, inbred passion and sense of urgency to Irish music that you don't find anywhere else in the world. It's part of their history, and it's what makes Irish rock so magical."

Irish Americans love a party, and large festivals like the Irish Fest in Milwaukee let them share their enthusiasm for music and dance.

Celebrations

Music and dance are often a part of Irish American celebrations. Most Irish American families will throw parties after important events such as a baptism, first communion, confirmation, wedding, or funeral. Food served may include traditional corned beef and cabbage, soda bread, an Irish stew, or smoked salmon, all favorite Irish American dishes. A dessert might be a double-crusted lemon tart with berries. But food is secondary to the singing and dancing at any Irish celebration.

Many Irish Americans also celebrate different saints' days, such as St. Brigid's Day or St. Joseph's Day, and, of course, St. Patrick's Day. Traditionally, these days are observed with a special mass or a quiet party at home,

Lexington Avenue in New York City, patrons of Tommy Makem's Irish Pavilion will launch enthusiastically into "Wish I Was a-Hunting" or "The Jolly Beggarman" — even though they're only two blocks from such stylishly American shops and stores as Bloomingdale's.

Traditional instrumental music is popular, too. This type of music usually involves such instruments as the harp, accordion, fiddle, flute, and tin whistle. Sadly, though the harp is a traditional symbol of Ireland, the ancient harp melodies have not survived. But much traditional Irish instrumental music has endured. It is often characterized by a haunting, lyrical quality and is

One Irish food that claims an enthusiastic following in America is soda bread, offered here for sampling at a fair.

though St. Patrick's Day has always been celebrated with a bit more noise.

St. Patrick's Day is a unique holiday in the United States because it belongs to a distinct ethnic group and yet is celebrated by the general population. As Finley Peter Dunne's fictional Mr. Dooley put it, "It's on'y on Pathrick's Day we can hire others to blow our horns f'r us." Dooley described this curious phenomenon:

> But ivrybody is an Irishman on Pathrick's Day. Schwartzmeister comes up wearin' a green cravat an' a yard long green badge an' says: 'Faugh-a-ballagh, Herr Dooley,' which he thinks is Irish f'r 'Good Mornin.' . . . Me good frind Ikey

Think "Irish," and the color green seems to come to mind. These festival goers have a wide assortment of merchandise to choose from, much of it green, and all of it proclaimed to be "Irish."

The St. Patrick's Day Parade in New York, like most St. Patrick's Day celebrations, extends far beyond the Irish American community in its appeal to many American groups.

THE IRISH WAKE

In most American traditions, the day before a funeral is the occasion of a solemn wake, where people pay their last respects to the one who has died and speak in hushed voices, consoling those left behind. Not so the Irish wake. Father Andrew M. Greeley has described the contemporary Irish American wake as "an extraordinary phenomenon, both heartless and reassuring, melancholy and rejoicing, unbearably painful and stubbornly hopeful." Irish Americans may acknowledge their loss and grief with loud keening, but they also celebrate their loved one's passing into a better world. At a traditional Irish wake, there will be jokes and stories told, singing and dancing, and, often, a great deal of alcohol consumed. A wake may last until the small hours of the morning or even go all night. Some may disapprove of such a party atmosphere, but at the center of it all, there is a deep conviction that death is not the end. And somehow, too, it is very Irish to defy death, even when it appears to have won.

Dorothy Hayden Cudahy basks in the limelight as Grand Marshal of the 1989 St. Patrick's Day Parade in New York. She was the first woman to lead this famous event.

Cohen jines me an' I observe he's left the glassware at home an' is wearin' emeralds in th' front iv his shirt. Like as not along will come little Hip Lung fr'm down th' sthreet with a package iv shirts undhr his ar-arm, an' a green ribbon in his cue.

St. Patrick's Day parades have been held in the United States since colonial days. No politician today, hoping for reelection, would dream of missing one. Some historians have linked Abram S. Hewitt's failure to be re-elected mayor of New York City in the late 1800s to his failure to fly the Irish flag on St. Patrick's Day. Today's celebrations include marathon runs, concerts, feasts, theatrical productions, children's programs, poetry readings, and various sporting events. Current traditions also include shamrock shakes at McDonald's, green bagels in many delicatessens, and green beer in the bars.

But there is a down side to St. Patrick's Day in America. Many Irish Americans are disgusted with the American emphasis on drinking alcohol as the primary means of celebrating St. Patrick's Day. Safety messages appear in newspapers and on television, and many cities offer free public transportation home for those who should not be driving. A few years ago, Leah Curtin, an active member of the St. Paul, Minnesota, Irish American community, started a national campaign to get Hallmark Cards and American Greetings to remove portraits of drunken Irishmen from

IRISH FOOD AND A RECIPE FOR IRISH STEW

The Irish do not have much of a distinctive cuisine, as many other ethnic groups do, possibly because of the long centuries their people ate little besides potatoes. But many people enjoy an Irish stew:

Ingredients:

1 pound boneless lamb, cut into two-inch cubes	two onions
1/4 cup flour	two stalks celery
2 teaspoons salt	three small carrots
a dash of pepper	three or four medium potatoes
	one medium turnip

Combine the flour, salt, and pepper and coat meat with the mixture. Brown coated meat in cooking oil, turning pieces occasionally. Drain fat and set aside. Bring one quart of water to a boil, add meat, and simmer forty-five minutes. Peel and clean vegetables. Cut into small pieces and add them to the stew with an extra teaspoon of salt and a dash of pepper. Cover and simmer another forty-five minutes or until food is tender. Remove meat and vegetables with slotted spoon and set aside. Add flour to cooking juice and stir until it thickens. Return meat and vegetables to pot and serve hot. Serves four.

their St. Patrick's Day cards. Ms. Curtin said, "St. Patrick founded no pubs, only churches, so there's no dignity in portraying drunken behavior as an activity in his honor." Both companies agreed to eliminate such portrayals from their cards.

Passion for the Past

Irish Americans have not just rediscovered their cultural past, they have also rediscovered their historic past, both individually and as a nation. Many Irish Americans have re-created their genealogies, or family trees, often going so far as to travel to Ireland to interview people and to pore over historic records. This is so popular a pastime among Irish Americans that special tours to Ireland are offered by travel agencies. Genealogy books abound, and nearly every Irish festival and cultural center offers genealogical help.

Part of the Irish American pride is also shown in the number of Irish festivals held each year in the United States and the number of Irish American organizations that flourish across this country. Dozens of cities across the nation annually host festivals featuring Irish music, Irish theatrical performances, Irish food, and an occasional contest for the reddest hair and the most freckles. Cultural centers provide a place for scholarly research, classes, activities, and exhibits. A recent issue of *The Irish American Post* listed several hundred meetings and social gatherings for midwesterners celebrating things Irish just in the month of March.

Stores specializing in Irish imports and Irish-theme merchandise thrive. There are Irish American radio stations and Irish American television programs. There is even a computer software program that allows the user to role-play the life of an Irish immigrant.

Concern for the Future

But the Irish in America do not care only about Irish history. Many are deeply concerned about current events in Ireland. For some, this means eagerly awaiting the latest soccer scores from Ireland, but for others, it means trying to help with the economic problems faced by the Republic of Ireland and concern over the "troubles" between Protestants and Catholics in Northern Ireland. The American Ireland Fund was founded by several prominent Irish American politicians to provide grants for community development, job training, education, and other social programs urgently needed in Ireland. The Irish Children's Fund brings Protestant and Catholic youth from Northern Ireland to the U.S. for a six-week visit, during which they can experience a lifestyle in which Protestants and Catholics live together in peace. Other Irish Americans have attempted to involve the United States in peace talks for Northern Ireland. They are, thus, continuing a long tradition of Irish loyalty.

Being Irish Means More than Drinking Green Beer

In Ireland, centuries of British oppression and scorn nearly wiped out the Celtic culture. In the United States, the desire of many Irish Americans to fit in and be accepted by native-born Americans caused them to turn their backs on Irish culture. A prominent sociologist once scornfully dismissed the Irish, claiming, "The Irish don't have a

This Bronx, New York, deli sells Irish papers. Irish Americans keep up with events in both the Republic of Ireland and Northern Ireland.

cultural heritage; they don't have a unique cuisine or an art or a family structure. They're just lower-middle-class WASPs [White, Anglo-Saxon Protestants] with a political style and a religious faith of their own." Fortunately, not all Irish Americans accepted this. They've kept alive the art, customs, and traditions rooted in their Celtic past. And culture in the United States has been greatly enriched by their discoveries and contributions. As one Irish American said with satisfaction, "There's more to being Irish than just drinking green beer on St. Patrick's Day."

One of the nation's most important, influential, and beloved Irish Americans was President John Fitzgerald Kennedy.

CHAPTER SIX

CONTRIBUTIONS TO AMERICAN CULTURE
IRISH AMERICAN ACHIEVEMENTS AND INFLUENCE

Irish Americans have participated in every aspect of American life. They went west with the goldrushers; worked as farmers, cowboys, ranchers, and trappers; built railroads and mined coal; served as peace officers and civil servants; headed large corporations and started small businesses; hit home runs and won Oscars; took in boarders, cleaned houses, and cared for children; skirted the law as professional gamblers and broke the law as outlaws and criminals. They gave us St. Patrick's Day, Irish stew, electrical circuits, the mass-produced automobile, and blarney for all occasions. The Irish have affected every part of American society.

Irish American Politicians

Nowhere has the impact of Irish America been greater than in American politics. The Irish have contributed many great American statesmen. First and foremost, of course, is John Fitzgerald Kennedy, thirty-fifth presi-

IRISH WORDS IN ENGLISH

Because the British tried to prevent the Irish from speaking Gaelic, most Irish immigrants spoke English when they came to America. Nevertheless, some Gaelic words have entered the English language.

Shamrock, *leprechaun*, and *banshee* all came from Gaelic words and have retained their original meaning. *Bother* came from an Irish word that meant "deaf," but in English it has changed to mean "to bewilder with noise." *Galore* came from the Irish "enough" and now means "abundant." It's fairly easy to imagine how these words changed their meaning, but it's hard to see how *fainnes*, which was Gaelic for "ring" became *phony*, which means "fake." Experts have traced that change to New York. Apparently, Irish immigrants tried to sell brass rings, which they called *fainnes*, to naive New Yorkers, claiming the rings were really gold. As buyers learned the *fainnes* were not gold, they declared the rings were *phony*.

Boycott is not a Gaelic word, but the Irish are responsible for its presence in the English language. In the late nineteenth century, Captain Charles C. Boycott angered the servants and agricultural workers on the estate he managed in County Mayo, Ireland, by refusing to lower rents. The servants and workers organized and refused to go to work. Their bold action was so admired that the word *boycott* has come to mean "refusing to deal with a person or group in order to express disapproval or to gain some concession." And the tactic has been adopted by other oppressed people.

JAMES SHIELDS

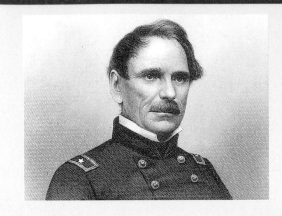

Irish American politician James Shields (1806?-1879) is the only American ever to have served three different states as senator. During his distinguished career, he was elected to the Senate from Illinois, Minnesota, and Missouri. He also served as governor of the Oregon Territory. Some historians have speculated that if he hadn't been Catholic, he might have been elected president.

Among the many prominent Irish Americans is former California governor Jerry Brown.

dent of the United States. Though Kennedy's term in office was tragically short, his magnetic appeal and his legacy of the Peace Corps still inspire idealistic people to give of themselves to help others. His encouragement of the space program led to the first moon landing and to many of today's technological advances.

But Kennedy is only one of the many Irish American statesmen who have served this country with distinction. Seventeen of our country's presidents can trace all or part of their ancestry to Ireland, though Kennedy is the only one with an Irish Catholic background. Three of the signers of the Declaration of Independence were born in Ireland; five were of Irish descent. Since 1776, the Irish Americans who have contributed significantly to American politics are far too numerous to list, but they include Alfred E. Smith, governor of New York; Robert F. Kennedy, U. S. attorney general and senator from New York; Richard J. Daley, mayor of Chicago; Mike Mansfield, Senate majority leader; John W. McCormick, Speaker of the House of Representatives; Eugene McCarthy, senator from Minnesota; Jerry Brown, governor of California; Thomas "Tip" O'Neill, Speaker of the House of Representatives; Edward Kennedy, senator from Massachusetts; Daniel P. Moynihan, U. S. ambassador to the United Nations and senator from New York; and many, many others.

Irish Americans have also served with distinction in the judicial system. Many have served as attorneys and judges, including two present-day Supreme Court justices — William G. Brennan and Sandra Day O'Connor, the first woman to serve on the Supreme Court.

But as important as the contributions of these individuals have been, the real impact Irish Americans have had on American politics has been in their approach to politics. Irish Americans dramatically changed the relationship between the government and its citizens.

Political Power

Irish immigrants saw political power as a tool to raise their people out of poverty. They were not interested in political theory or ideas. In Ireland, they had seen the British use the government to steal their land and grant privileges to English Protestants. In

Irish American Sandra Day O'Connor is the first woman appointed to the U.S. Supreme Court.

America, they were determined to seize some of that kind of power for themselves and use it for their own people.

Irish immigrants were attracted primarily to the Democratic party because of its openness to people of different backgrounds. At first, they provided a large voting block in return for jobs and services. But they were not content to stay in the lower ranks of the party. Irish Americans worked their way up from precinct captains to ward leaders to aldermen, eventually controlling most city governments in the northern United States and New Orleans in the South.

AN UNUSUAL FRIENDSHIP

Today, as in the past, many Irish Americans in public service see people in need as human beings, not statistics, and have proved willing to go beyond the strict limits of their job descriptions to help. In 1973 in New York City, a young African American woman named Pat Johnson was hit by five bullets fired by a gunman in a passing car. Police believed that her life was still in danger after the incident, so she was put in the Witness Protection Program.

One of the police detectives assigned to her case was a fifty-year-old Irish American cop, Jimmy Mulvey. Ms. Johnson had been left disabled and nearly blind by the shooting, but her remarkably strong will kept her struggling to recover. As Jimmy watched her struggle, a friendship and mutual respect developed between them. Jimmy encour-aged Pat to relearn such skills as cooking and to keep going when things got rough. She remembers he once yelled at her, "Don't ever say *can't* to me!" when she wanted to quit. Once Jimmy and his wife bought Pat a new dress and took her out dancing. Their families shared birthday and holiday celebrations.

The friendship Jimmy offered went far beyond simply providing protection and continued after Pat's need for police protection ended, until Jimmy's death in 1989. Even today, Pat still travels once a month to visit Jimmy's kids, her "other family." Jimmy Mulvey's Irish American gift of seeing others as human beings, not "cases," provided a benefit to his own family and to Pat and her family — and provides an example for the whole human race.

Patronage

Once in positions of power, Irish Americans used their power to provide benefits for family and friends. Irish Americans did not regard this as corruption. In Ireland, people were accustomed to swapping a sack of potatoes in return for help with planting a field. In America, an alderman might help someone's son get a job and that person would then sign a petition or contribute to a campaign. An Irish American cop might ignore a food vendor's violations of city ordinances, and that food vendor would then cast his ballot the "right" way. Author and politician George Reedy recalls that when he needed a summer job, his alderman wrote a letter to get him hired at Riverview, a Chicago amusement park. Political analyst Tim Russert recalled an alderman winning two thousand dollars in a card game and giving that money to Russert so he could attend law school.

The Irish American patronage system allowed both parties to keep their self-respect. The alderman did not regard the services he provided as charity and did not treat the recipients as inferior. Both parties simply had a business deal: political support traded for social services. Irish American politicians did not hold themselves above the people they served. They were in the neighborhood, sharing the joy of a baptism or bar mitzvah, or the sorrow of a funeral. Before Franklin D. Roosevelt's New Deal (crafted partly by Irish Americans) helped people, the government provided little relief for the poor. Instead, Irish American politicians provided that much needed service — and did so treating those in need with dignity and respect.

Mayor of Chicago for over two decades, Richard J. Daley used the patronage system to make Chicago the "City that Works."

Unfortunately, however, many Irish American politicians abused the power they had won. Bribery, kickbacks, and graft were commonplace. Elections were often rigged. A common joke ran, "Vote early, vote often," and some did. Many times, payoffs determined who would receive city contracts. Roads and public buildings were often built on property owned by politicians and their friends, allowing the owners to make large profits. Some benefits intended for the poor were not awarded based on need, but rather on a person's political connections. Greed often overtook compassion. Many Irish American politicians amassed large personal fortunes; some eventually served jail terms.

A Rich Legacy

But the legacy of Irish American politicians is more positive than negative. Irish Americans were the first to use the government as a vehicle for redistribution of wealth, the first in America to use political power to help the powerless. At first, they provided food and jobs for the poor on an individual basis. Eventually, they passed the laws that set up the modern welfare system, providing help and protection for the underprivileged.

Irish Americans introduced America to practical politics. They were not interested in abstract philosophy; they were interested in getting things done. People frequently criticized Mayor Richard J. Daley, a typical Irish American politician, but they acknowledged that Chicago under his administration was the "City that Worked." There weren't a lot of ethical reforms, but streets were plowed, garbage was picked up, and civil service strikes were avoided.

THE CONGRESSIONAL MEDAL OF HONOR

The Congressional Medal of Honor, has been awarded to 257 Irish Americans, more than twice the number awarded any other ethnic group.

Irish Americans were also the architects of the political coalition. Though Irish American politicians were primarily interested in helping other Irish Americans, they did provide significant help to African Americans and various other ethnic groups — in return for votes. Irish Americans succeeded as no other group has in getting diverse and often hostile groups to cooperate with one another.

Most Irish Americans today are still more practical than philosophical in their politics. When Tim Russert was asked why he supported politician Daniel P. Moynihan, he replied simply, "I thought he could win." Winners stand a chance of accomplishing something; losers, even if their goals are noble, are just losers. As a result, many of today's upper-middle-class Irish Americans now vote Republican instead of Democratic.

But however they vote, they are likely to be intensely interested in politics. According to sociologist Andrew Greeley, "The Irish are the most politically active of American ethnic groups. They are more likely to campaign, to contribute money to politics, to vote, to join civic organizations, [and] to contact a political leader."

The politics that emerged from the Irish immigrant urban ghettoes have broadened the base of political power in the United States and extended the benefits of that power to reach more Americans, regardless of their race, religion, or economic status.

Labor Unions

Irish Americans became involved with labor unions for many of the same reasons they became involved in politics. There were few, if any, laws to protect workers in the late nineteenth and early twentieth centuries. Irish Americans helped organize and support unions that put pressure on employers to deal with employees fairly. They participated in local unions and became active in national organizations, such as the Knights of Labor and the American Federation of Labor.

Just as they did in the political system, Irish Americans rose quickly to positions of power within these organizations. Their efforts helped workers gain job security, higher wages, shorter workdays, and safer working conditions. Irish Americans, such as George Meany, head of the AFL-CIO for more than twenty years, and Mary Harris, the "Miner's Angel," were among those who worked tirelessly to improve the lot of the average worker.

Builders of America

The lot of the average worker desperately needed improving, especially by the early twentieth century. As nineteenth-century America switched from an agricultural to an industrial nation, a vast supply of cheap labor was needed to staff the factories, mine coal for energy, and build transportation systems to get goods to markets. African American slave labor required a large investment of money, so industrialists were reluctant to use them for really dangerous work. But there seemed to be an endless supply of Irish laborers, and so industrialists used them (and other "expendable" ethnic groups such as the Chinese) to dig canals, build railroads, and drain mosquito-infested swamps.

Some historians have claimed one

Irishman died for every railroad tie laid in America. It is estimated that between eight thousand and thirty thousand Irish Americans died digging the New Basin Canal near New Orleans. Countless others died in construction accidents or from diseases, such as malaria and black lung disease, contracted in their work environments. Irish Americans supplied much of the labor that built America's cities and its transportation system, but the cost in lives was incalculable.

The Irish Mob

Not all of Irish America's contributions to American society have been on the right side of the law. The despair of some of the early Irish immigrants led them into crime. Irish gangs formed in the slums of many American cities. Though time altered the circumstances of most Irish Americans, the gangs did not disappear. The gangs became organized mobs involved in extortion, kidnapping, the numbers racket, and other criminal activities. The police had difficulty investigating these crimes because of the strong loyalty the individuals in the neighborhoods had toward one another, whether they were involved or not.

One of the most notorious of these mobs operated in Hell's Kitchen in New York City. Christened the "Westies" by the press, this mob, led by Jimmy Coonan, was responsible for many vicious murders and a

One of boxing's greatest fighters, Jack Dempsey held the world heavyweight boxing championship from 1919 to 1926.

reign of terror that lasted several decades. Coonan and several of his henchmen were finally arrested and convicted in 1988 when Micky Featherstone, a member of the mob, turned against them and became a police informer.

Professional Sports

While some Irish Americans escaped the lot of the majority by entering politics, others became priests, nuns, or monks. Other roads

Colorful tennis great John McEnroe.

to be so prominent in the sport that some non-Irish boxers adopted Irish-sounding names.

Boxing excellence did little to improve the image of Irish Americans in the eye of the American public, but their participation in the most American of American sports, baseball, helped speed their entry into mainstream American life. Irish Americans fell in love with baseball, and their grace and skill on the baseball diamond made Irish American ball players heroes to the entire nation. One historian has estimated that in the early 1900s more than 90 percent of all professional baseball players were Irish or German. Irish American Charles Albert Comiskey founded the Chicago White Sox in 1900. And Irish American Cornelius McGillicuddy (better known as Connie Mack) is acknowledged as one of the greatest baseball managers of all time.

Today, Irish Americans can be found in just about any professional sport, though no longer in the numbers they once were. The "Fighting Irish," Notre Dame's football team, now includes many ethnic and racial groups. But there are still Irish Americans making a name for themselves in sports, such as Jimmy Connors and John McEnroe, top-ranked tennis players; Ben Hogan and Sam Snead, among the greatest golfers ever to have played; and golfer Meg Mallon, 1991 Sportswoman of the Year.

of escape were also open to some Irish Americans: professional sports and the entertainment business.

Boxing attracted many Irish immigrants and their descendants, and in the late nineteenth century and early twentieth century, Irish American champions dominated the sport. Prizefighters such as "Gentleman Jim" Corbett, Jack Dempsey, and John L. Sullivan provided role models and heroes for the Irish American community. Irish Americans grew

"There's No Business Like Show Business"

Irish Americans also gained prominence in the field of entertainment. Irish charm and wit are legendary, and Irish Americans have put both to good use making careers for themselves as actors, singers, dancers, directors, and producers.

Irish Americans were prominent in vaudeville during the early part of the century, the most famous star being George M. Cohan, actor, author, director, and composer of such songs as "Yankee Doodle Dandy," "Give My Regards to Broadway," and "Over There." Irish dancing in vaudeville was one of the most importance influences to shape modern tap dancing, and it inspired some of the great production numbers that characterized early musicals.

Irish America gave Hollywood some of its greatest stars, including James Cagney, Bing Crosby, Helen Hayes, Buster Keaton, Grace Kelly, Gene Kelly, Mary Tyler Moore, Carroll O'Connor, Donald O'Connor, Maureen O'Hara, Gregory Peck, Mickey Rourke, Ed Sullivan, Spencer Tracy, and John Wayne. The Irish American family of the Barrymores,

including Lionel, Ethel, John, and Diana Barrymore, performed with great distinction on both the Broadway stage and in movies, a tradition carried into the current generation by actress Drew Barrymore.

Literature

Given the Irish love of words and knowledge, the Irish American community has produced fewer authors than one might expect. Many historians have attributed this to the Irish American hunger for security. Par-

Actress Mary Tyler Moore contributes her time to charitable organizations such as the Juvenile Diabetes Foundation. Here, she testifies before a House subcommittee requesting funding for research into juvenile diabetes.

Actress Drew Barrymore continues the show business tradition of her family. In this 1985 photo, she is shown presenting actor Emmanuel Lewis a People's Choice Award.

IRISH THEMES: A HIT AT HOME AND AT THE BOX OFFICE

In the hit movie *Robocop,* a fatally wounded police officer, Alex Murphy, is saved by scientists who place his brain in a robot, creating a cyborg. In *Robocop 2,* experiments trying to duplicate Robocop fail. A character explains why Murphy succeeded in making the adjustment while others couldn't: "Alex Murphy — top of his class — devout Irish Catholic — family man — everything in his profile indicates a fierce sense of duty." Irish Americans have come a long way from the days of "No Irish Need Apply."

Everywhere, popular culture today tells the same story: Irish Americans are an admired and influential segment of American society. The hit TV show of the 1993-94 television season was "NYPD Blue," starring a sensitive, compassionate, red-haired Irish American cop, played by David Caruso. The 1992 Tony Award for Best Play went to *Dancing at Lughnasa,* a story about five Irish sisters. That same year saw Tom Cruise star in *Far and Away,* a movie about the experiences of two Irish immigrants.

Science fiction/fantasy books containing Celtic themes abound, including internationally best-selling author Morgan Llywelyn's novels *Lion of Ireland: The Legend of Brian Boru* and *Finn MacCool.* A 1993 Academy Award nominee for Best Picture was *In the Name of the Father,* a movie telling the true story of an innocent Irish man who served fifteen years in jail, convicted of an IRA bombing because British police deliberately falsified evidence against him.

ents who had suffered poverty might encourage their children to read books, but they steered them to choose "practical" careers. Nevertheless, some still chose to write, and these Irish Americans have given us some great works of literature and some wonderful entertainment.

Many of the first Irish American writers were journalists. Nellie Bly, a famous reporter and crusader, gained international attention when she wrote about her journey around the world in less than eighty days. Finley Peter Dunne wrote essays that were both history and political commentary. His most famous character, Mr. Dooley, provided witty political insights and brought to life the Chicago Irish American neighborhood of Bridgeport. Modern Irish American journalists, such as Pete Hamill and Pulitzer Prize-winner Jimmy Breslin, continue the tradition of Irish American journalistic excellence.

Irish American Eugene O'Neill is considered by many to be the greatest playwright of this century. Winner of several Pulitzer Prizes and the Nobel Prize for literature, he wrote primarily about tortured family relationships. (*Ah! Wilderness* was the only play he wrote that wasn't a tragedy.) His *Long Day's Journey into Night, Moon for the Misbegotten,* and *The Iceman Cometh* rank among the finest plays ever written and helped influence the American theater's movement toward realism.

Irish American F. Scott Fitzgerald is considered one of the century's greatest novelists. He provided a glittering, yet realistic, portrait of the Jazz Age in such novels as *Tender is the Night, This Side of Paradise,* and *The Great Gatsby.* James T. Farell's many novels, including the *Studs Lonigan* trilogy, provided a harsh yet sympathetic view of Chicago's South Side Irish during and after the Depres-

Elizabeth Cochrane Seaman, better known as Nellie Bly, gained international fame in 1889 when she wrote of her trip around the world in seventy-two days, six hours, eleven minutes, and fourteen seconds.

Journalist Jimmy Breslin won the Pulitzer Prize for commentary in 1986.

Novelist F. Scott Fitzgerald is considered by many to be among the greatest American writers. Known as the spokeman of the Jazz Age, his works vividly preserve the frenzy and spiritual poverty he saw as typical of the era.

sion years. Many modern Irish American novels have also dealt with the experience of being Irish: some with bitterness, such as Mary Gordon's *Other Side;* some with humor, such as John Power's *Last Catholic in America* and *Do Black Patent Leather Shoes Really Reflect Up?;* and some with compassionate realism, such as Jimmy Breslin's *World Without End, Amen.* Edwin O'Connor ex- plored the world of the Irish American Catholic Church in his Pulitzer Prize-winning novel *The Edge of Sadness* and Irish American politics in *The Last Hurrah.* Other important and influential Irish American writers include Edward Hannibal, Maureen Howard, William Kennedy, Flannery O'Connor, John O'Hara, Anne McCaffrey, and Mary McCarthy.

Business and Industry

A wit once said, "The only place in Ireland where a man can make a fortune is America." Indeed, some Irish Americans have amassed great fortunes in business and contributed to the growth of American industry at the same time. William Randolph Hearst founded the largest newspaper chain in America. Andrew Mellon made millions in a variety of business enterprises. His art collection, donated to the government, was the foundation for the National Gallery of Art. Joseph Kennedy amassed a fortune in banking and the stock market. Stockbroker James Francis McDonnell determined he would make a million dollars for each of his fourteen children — and he did. Inventor Thomas E. Murray, who held over eleven hundred patents, made a fortune by inventing the circuits, switches, and power systems that got electricity into his partner Thomas Edison's invention, the incandescent light bulb. Currently, Irish American Tony O'Reilly is keeping alive the tradition of the shrewd Irish businessman as president of the H. J. Heinz Co.

An Intangible Legacy

On balance, the concrete contributions of Irish Americans to American society have been numerous and significant. Yet perhaps their most important contributions have been intangible. Irish Americans have tremendous vitality, a fierce faith in life, and a

Author Mary Gordon writes of the modern Irish American experience.

passion for freedom. Though their ancestors suffered a thousand years of British oppression, they never gave up. They kept living and loving and believing that tomorrow would be a better day. Irish Americans brought these qualities to America, and all America is richer for them.

AN IRISH PROVERB

"An inch is a great deal on a nose."

CHRONOLOGY

300 B.C. The Celts settle in Ireland.

A.D. 432 St. Patrick converts Ireland to Christianity.

795 The Vikings invade Ireland.

1014 The Irish drive out the Vikings.

1171 King Henry II of England lands troops in southern Ireland and conquers the land.

1534 King Henry VIII of England breaks with the Catholic Church and establishes the Church of England. He tries to force the Irish to renounce their loyalty to the Catholic Church, but the majority refuse.

1601 Elizabeth I of England violently suppresses Irish rebellion.

1690 Oliver Cromwell violently suppresses Irish Catholic rebels in the Battle of Boyne.

1719 Many of the most repressive of the Penal Laws are passed, including laws banishing all Catholic bishops from Ireland under penalty of death, laws prohibiting Catholics from voting, and laws forbidding Catholics to open schools of their own or send their children abroad for an education.

1829 Repeal of the Penal Laws.

1844 An anti-Catholic, anti-Irish riot in Philadelphia leaves forty dead and sixty seriously wounded; property damage includes the destruction of eighty-one houses, two Catholic churches, two rectories, two convents, and a Catholic library.

1845–1855 A blight destroys most of the Irish potato crop, bringing extreme famine on the land; nearly two million Irish choose to emigrate to North America to avoid starvation.

1849 Some Irish immigrants join the California gold rush; a few strike it rich.

1853 An ad in the *Daily Sun* reads: "Woman wanted to do general housework . . . English, Scotch, Welsh, German, or any country or color except Irish."

1861–1865 Many Irish immigrants enlist in the army during the U.S. Civil War; their courage and bravery help begin a change in the attitudes of native-born Americans and start some Irish immigrants toward assimilation into the general population.

1875 John McCloskey is appointed the first American cardinal of Irish descent for the Catholic Church.

1889 Irish American Nellie Bly gains international attention when she travels around the world in seventy-two days, six hours, eleven minutes, and fourteen seconds.

1892 Irish American John L. Sullivan captures the world heavyweight boxing championship.

1900 Charles Albert Comisky founds the Chicago White Sox.

1916 The Irish rebel against British rule in Ireland with the "Easter Rising"; the ruthless suppression of the rebellion by the British military prompts many Irish Americans to work to stir international sympathy for Ireland, forcing Britain to reconsider its Irish policy.

1921 Ireland receives dominion status from Britain, forming the Irish Free State. Six counties remain under British control as Northern Ireland.

1925 F. Scott Fitzgerald publishes *The Great Gatsby*.

1928 Alfred E. Smith, a Democrat, is the first Irish Catholic to be nominated for president of the United States.

1935 James T. Farrell publishes the *Studs Lonigan* trilogy.

1936 Eugene O'Neill is awarded the Nobel Prize for Literature.

1938	Spencer Tracy receives his second Best Actor Oscar for his portrait of a priest in *Boys Town*.
1940	Congress awards George M. Cohan a special medal for his World War I patriotic song, "Over There."
1942	Bing Crosby records "White Christmas" for the movie *Holiday Inn;* the song wins an Oscar and becomes the best-selling single of all time.
1949	The Irish Free State breaks all ties with Britain, forming the Republic of Ireland.
1950	The Irish Institute is founded in New York is to preserve Irish customs, arts, and culture in America.
1953	Golfer Ben Hogan wins his fourth U.S. Open and second Masters Tournaments.
1960	John F. Kennedy is elected president of the U.S., the first Irish American Catholic to hold that office.
1971	*The Irish World,* the oldest Irish American weekly newspaper, celebrates its first one hundred years.
1977	Representative Thomas "Tip" O'Neill is elected Speaker of the House of Representatives.
1978	Mary Gordon publishes *Final Payments;* it becomes a surprise best seller.
1981	Sandra Day O'Connor is appointed the first woman on the U.S. Supreme Court.
1984	John McEnroe wins his fourth U.S. Open Tennis Championship.
1986	Jimmy Breslin is awarded the Pulitzer Prize for Journalism.
1988	The Irish American mob known as the "Westies" is broken up when one of its members turns informant and many of its members are convicted of crimes including murder, kidnapping, and racketeering.
1992	*Dancing at Lughnasa,* a play about five Irish sisters, receives the Tony Award for Best Play.
1993	*In the Name of the Father* receives seven nominations for Academy Awards.

GLOSSARY

Alderman   An elected city official who serves under a mayor in the city legislative body.

Almshouse   A home for the poor operated by a private organization.

Baptism   A sacrament practiced by a Christian church in which a person is sprinkled with or immersed in water, representing that that person has been cleansed of his or her sins and is part of the Christian community.

Bard   A person who composes and recites stories, usually of heroic warriors and their deeds; these stories are often composed as songs or poetry.

Blarney   Skillful flattery or nonsensical speech.

Blight   A disease that attacks plants resulting in parts of the plant ceasing to grow or withering away.

Bodhran   A percussion instrument similar to a drum.

Catechism   Statements summarizing religious beliefs or doctrine, often phrased as questions and answers.

Clan   A group of families who trace their descent from a common ancestor.

Communion   A sacrament of the Christian church in which bread and wine are consumed in remembrance of the last supper and crucifixion of Jesus.

Estate	A large section of residential property, usually containing a mansion.
Eviction	A legal process whereby tenants are forced to vacate their homes, usually for not paying rent.
Graft	Gaining money or privilege by questionable or dishonest means.
Hurling	An Irish team sport similar to field hockey or lacrosse.
Indentured servant	A person who formally agrees to work for another person for a given period of time in return for some consideration, such as payment of passage allowing that person to immigrate.
Keen	A loud, wailing cry, often a lament for the dead.
Land agent	A person who manages rental property for a landlord.
Liturgy	A ritualized ceremony in public worship that often involves recitation of religious beliefs.
Mass	A public worship service that includes a celebration of communion.
Parish	An area or neighborhood served by a single pastor.
Patronage	The power to award privileges or government jobs on a basis other than merit.
Peat bog	An area of marshy ground formed by partially decomposed plants.
Quarantine	To place a person or group of people in isolation for a specified period of time; this is often done to attempt to control the spread of disease.
Rosary beads	A string of beads used by Roman Catholics to count prayers.
Runners	Con artists who tried to exploit immigrants by selling them expensive, often useless, goods and directing them to specific boarding houses whose landlords continue to exploit them.
Sacrament	A sacred, ritualized ceremony.
Shanty	A small, poorly-built shelter.
Steerage	The least expensive passage in a ship; often passengers were accommodated in cargo holds.
Thatch	A strawlike plant material often used for a roof on small cottages.
Wake	A gathering of friends and relatives before the burial of a person where the people view the body and, often, celebrate his or her passage into a new and hopefully better life.

FURTHER READING

Brownstein, Robin, and Peter Guttmacher. *The Scotch-Irish Americans.* New York: Chelsea House, 1988.

Callahan, Bob, ed. *The Big Book of American Irish Culture.* New York: Viking Penguin Books, 1987.

Conlon-McKenna, Marita. *Wildflower Girl.* New York: Holiday House, 1991.

Cooper, Brian E. *The Irish American Almanac and Green Pages.* New York: Harper and Row, 1990.

Davis, Courtney. *The Celtic Art Source Book.* New York: Sterling Publishing Co., 1988.

Haas, Dorothy. *My First Communion.* Niles, Ill.: Albert Whitman and Co., 1987.

Kelleher, Margaret. *So You Think You're Irish.* New York: Wing Books, 1988.

Meyer, Carolyn. *Voices of Northern Ireland.* San Diego: Harcourt, Brace, Jovanovich, 1987.

Morpurgo, Michael. *Twist of Gold.* New York: Viking, 1993.

Nardo, Don. *The Irish Potato Famine.* San Diego: Lucent Books, 1990.

Nixon, Joan Lowery. *Land of Promise.* New York: Bantam Books, 1993.

Watts, J. F. *The Irish Americans.* New York: Chelsea House, 1988.

INDEX

Abortion, 44
AFL-CIO, 68
African American Aylo Children's Dance
    Theatre, 55
African Americans, 68
Alcohol, 13, 30, 58, 59-60
American culture, mainstream; Irish
    Americans' contributions to, 51-60,
    63-75
American Federation of Labor, 68
American Indians, 9
American Ireland Fund, 61
Art, 48, 50, 61, 71-75
Assimilation, 24, 25, 33-34, 35, 43-44,
    61
Atlantic Ocean, 8, 19
Automobile, invention of, 23

Ballinglass, 13
Barrymore family, 71
Barrymore, Drew, 72
Belfast, 12
Birmingham, Stephen, 33
Birth control, 29, 44
Blarney, 52
Blarney Stone, 52
Bly, Nellie, 73
Book of Kells, The, 51, 53
Boston, 16, 20, 23, 33, 38
Boycott, Charles C., 63
Brennan, William G., 65
Breslin, Jimmy, 73, 74
Britain (British), 7, 8-9, 10, 12, 13-14,
    15, 20, 22, 24, 27, 32, 37, 38, 41,
    50, 51, 52, 54, 61, 63, 65, 72, 75
Bronx, 32, 35, 41, 61
Brown, Jerry, 64, 65
Buffalo, 27
Business, 75

Cagney, James, 71
California, 65
Canada, 12, 18, 20
Carey, Hugh, 25
Carthy, Cormac, 52
Caruso, David, 72
Celebrations, 12-13, 36, 56, 58
Celtic culture, 50, 51-53, 61
Celts, 27, 28
Chicago, 40, 44, 54, 55, 65, 67, 73
Chicago White Sox, 70
Chieftains, the, 55
Children, 10, 25, 27, 29, 30, 45, 46
China (Chinese), 68
Cinnamons, 56
Civil War, 22
Claddagh Ring, 53

Clark, Mary Higgins, 29, 31, 49, 50, 55
Clergy marriage, 44
Coffin ships, 18, 19
Cohan, George M., 71
Comiskey, Charles Albert, 70
Communication, patterns of, 30-31
Congressional Medal of Honor, 68
Connors, Jimmy, 70
Conversion, 14, 25, 37, 38
Coonan, Jimmy, 69
Corbett, "Gentleman Jim," 70
Coulter, Phil, 55
County Cork, 23, 52
County Donegal, 6
County Mayo, 63
County Meath, 51
Crime, 20, 21, 69
Crosby, Bing, 71
Cruise, Tom, 72
Cudahy, Dorothy Hayden, 59
Curtin, Leah, 59

Daley, Richard J., 65, 67
Dance, 12, 48, 53-55, 56, 71
Dearborn, 23
De Beaumont (traveler), 9
Declaration of Independence, 64
Democratic party, 22, 65, 68
Dempsey, Jack, 69, 70
Detroit, 23
DeVere, Stephen, 19
Discrimination, 21-22, 24, 32, 33, 37,
    40, 41
Disease, 7, 19, 20, 21, 22, 69
Divorce, 44
Dublin, 12, 43, 51
Dunne, Finley Peter, 20, 21, 57, 73

East Coast, 17, 33
Eastern Europe (Eastern Europeans), 42
Education, 9, 40, 50
Elizabeth and Sarah, 19
Elizabeth I, 41, 52
Emotions, expressing, 29-30
England (English). *See* Britain (British)
English language, 22, 25, 52, 63
Entertainment, 71
Europe (Europeans), 8, 18, 37, 54. *See
    also specific nations*
Evictions, 10, 11, 13

Family: goals of, 32-33, 71; roles in, 27-
    29
Farell, James T., 73
Farming, 6, 10, 12, 14, 23
Featherstone, Micky, 69
Feminism, 28

Festivals, 26, 28, 33, 55, 56, 57, 60
Fishing, 12
Fitz and the Celts, 55, 56
Fitzgerald, F. Scott, 73, 74
Fleming (immigrant), 25
Fleming, Thomas (novelist), 29
Food, 14, 49, 56, 57, 60, 63
Ford, Henry, 23
Ford, John, 23
France (French), 42

Gaelic, 8, 9, 22, 35, 50, 63
Garden State Ceili Band, 55
Genealogy, 60
German Americans, 42, 70
Germany (Germans), 42
Gerrard, Mrs. (landlord), 13
Ghillies, the, 56
Gordon, Mary, 74, 75
Greeley, Andrew, 29, 31, 34, 58, 68
Grosse Isle, 20

Hamill, Pete, 55, 73
Hannibal, Edward, 74
Harris, Mary, 68
Hayes, Helen, 71
Hearst, William Randolph, 75
Hedge schools, 9, 40
Henry II, 8
Henry VIII, 8, 37
Hewitt, Abram S., 59
Hogan, Ben, 70
Hospitality, 13, 49-50
Housework, 34
Housing: in Ireland, 9-10, 11; in U.S.,
    20, 21, 32, 33-34
Howard, Maureen, 74
Howard, Ron, 54

Illinois, 64
Immigrants, 8, 15, 16, 17-24, 27, 31,
    34, 38, 41, 42, 47, 50, 63, 65, 69;
    arrival of, 21, 37; distribution of,
    17; life of, 17, 19, 20-25, 31, 33;
    work of, 22
Immigration, 7-8, 12, 15; conditions of,
    18-20
Ireland (Irish), 6-15, 17, 19, 22, 26, 31,
    35, 37-38, 39, 43, 49, 50, 51, 53,
    54, 60, 61, 64, 65; climate of, 10;
    history of, 7-10, 13-15, 27, 51; life
    in, 7-15, 17, 21
Irish Children's Fund, 61
Italy (Italians), 42

Jersey City, 25
Johnson, Pat, 66

Joyce, James, 51
Joyce, Richard, 53
Judicial system, 13, 65

Keaton, Buster, 71
Kelly, Grace, 71
Kelly, Gene, 71
Kennedy, Edward "Ted," 32, 65
Kennedy, John F., 25, 32, 33, 43, 62, 63-64
Kennedy, Joseph, 75
Kennedy, Robert F., 32, 65
Kennedy, Rose, 33
Kennedy, William, 74
Kenny, Tony, 55
Knights of Labor, 68

Labor unions, 24, 68
Lace curtain Irish, 34
Landlords, 8-9, 10, 13, 14
Lent, 46
Lewis, Emmanuel, 72
Llywelyn, Morgan, 72
London, 13, 52
Loyalty, 26, 27, 35, 50, 61

Mack, Connie, 70
Maine, 8
Mallon, Meg, 70
Mansfield, Mike, 65
Marriage, 10, 31
Massachusetts, 35, 65
McCaffrey, Anne, 74
McCarthy, Eugene, 65
McCarthy, Mary, 74
McCormick, Bernard, 29, 34
McCormick, John W., 65
McDonnell, James Francis, 75
McEnroe, John, 70
McGillicuddy, Cornelius, 70. See Mack, Connie
McTavish, 56
Meany, George, 68
Media, 60
Mellon, Andrew, 75
Men's roles, 25, 27, 28, 29
Michigan, 23
Midwest, 17, 33, 50
Migration to U.S. West, 23
Military, Irish Americans in, 22, 24, 33
Milwaukee, 54, 55, 56
Minnesota, 59, 64, 65
Missouri, 64
Molly Maguires, 24
Moore, Mary Tyler, 71
Movies, 54, 72
Moynihan, Daniel P., 65, 68

Mulvey, Jimmy, 66
Murray, Thomas E., 75
Music, 49, 55, 56, 60
Myths, 51-52

Names, 25
Nashville, 54
National Gallery of Art, 75
Neighborhoods, 34-35, 43
New Deal, 66
New Hampshire, 22
New Jersey, 28, 55
New Orleans, 16, 20, 34-35, 38, 65, 69
New York (city), 15, 16, 20, 22, 30, 31, 35, 36, 38, 39, 45, 49, 52, 56, 59, 63, 66, 69
New York (state), 22, 27, 61, 65
Newspapers, 50, 52, 75
Northern Ireland, 41, 61
Nuns, 38, 40, 42, 43, 44, 69

O'Connor, Carroll, 71
O'Connor, Donald, 71
O'Connor, Edwin, 74
O'Connor, Flannery, 74
O'Connor, Sandra Day, 65
O'Hara, John, 74
O'Hara, Maureen, 71
O'Neill, Eugene, 73
O'Neill, Thomas "Tip," 65
O'Reilly, Tony, 75
Oregon Territory, 64

Parochial Schools, 40
Patrick, Saint, 37, 38, 39, 60
Patronage, 66-67
Peasants, 8-10, 13
Peat, 10
Peck, Gregory, 71
Penal Laws, 8, 9, 32, 37
Pennsylvania, 22
Philadelphia, 41
Politics, 22, 24, 32, 35, 50, 59, 63-68, 69
Pope: allegiance to, 42, 44; fear of, 21, 22
Potato famine, 7, 14-15, 18, 29, 31, 32, 49
Potter, George, 17
Power, John, 74
Prayers, 43, 47
Prejudice. See Discrimination
Priests, 28, 37, 38, 40, 42, 43, 44, 45, 46, 69
Proverbs, 32, 75

Quebec, 20

Rebellions, 13, 24
Reedy, George, 66
Religion: Catholicism (Catholics), 8, 12, 21-22, 25, 28, 29, 32, 33, 36-47, 50, 61, 64, 74; Protestantism (Protestants), 8, 21, 25, 37, 41, 61, 65
Republican party, 68
Rome, 44
Roosevelt, Franklin D., 52, 66
Rourke, Mickey, 71
Runners, 21
Russert, Tim, 27, 66, 68

Sacraments, 45-47; baptism, 45-46; confession, 46; Confirmation, 46; First Communion, 46; of the Sick, 47; wedding, 47
Saints, 56
Scotch Irish. See Religion: Protestantism (Protestants)
Second Vatican Council, 44
Secret societies, 24
Self-esteem, 33
Shamrocks, 39
Shanty Irish, 34, 41
Shields, James, 64
Skibbereen, 7
Slavery, 9, 68
Smith, Alfred E., 64
Snead, Sam, 70
Social services, 40, 41, 42, 43, 66, 67
South, 41, 65
Sports, 12, 24, 30, 35, 37, 50, 70
Springfield, 35
Storytelling, 51, 52
St. Patrick's Day, 36, 56-57, 58, 59-60, 61, 63
St. Paul, 59
Sullivan, Ed, 71
Sullivan, John L., 70

Theater, 60, 72
Tracy, Spencer, 71
Traditions, 13, 26, 27, 30, 35, 61
Trinity Dance Company, 54, 55

U2, 56

Wakes, 58
Walker, Jimmy, 52
Wayne, John, 71
West, 33
Women's roles, 27-29, 40, 44
Work, 25, 44, 50, 63, 68-69
World Cup, 30
Writers, 51-53, 71, 72, 73-74